TEACHING WITHOUT LOSING YOUR MIND

Practical Strategies to Lead Your Classroom,

Build Better Routines,

and Stop the Chaos

For Grades 6–9

Xiomara Granado-Ramos, M.Ed.

TEACHING WITHOUT LOSING YOUR MIND

Practical Strategies to Lead Your Classroom,

Build Better Routines,

and Stop the Chaos

For Grades 6–9

ISBN: 979-8-9875469-8-7 (Paperback)

Published in the United States of America

DEDICATION

For every teacher trying to make it through the year—
you do not have to be perfect to be the teacher your students need.

ACKNOWLEDGMENTS

First, I give thanks to Yahweh for His guidance, strength, and faithfulness throughout the writing of this book. Thank you to my husband, David, for his love, support, and encouragement. I am also deeply grateful to my children, who are my greatest motivation. I could not have done this without them.

TABLE OF CONTENTS

Introduction

Why This Book Exists

I did not write this book because I had everything figured out. I wrote it because I know how hard teaching can feel when you care deeply, work hard, and still struggle to lead the room in front of you.

When I first started teaching, I thought being a good teacher meant having solid lessons, being prepared, and caring about students. Those things matter. But I learned very quickly that without classroom management, even a good lesson can fall apart.

That is especially true in Grades 6–9, when students are still learning consistency, self-control, and responsibility. We are not just teaching content. We are also teaching students how to function in school: how to enter the room, follow routines, respond to structure, and meet expectations.

When expectations are unclear and routines are weak, teachers end up reacting all day instead of leading. And that makes everything harder than it needs to be.

That is why this book exists.

I wrote it for teachers who want something practical—not a long book full of theory or abstract advice that sounds good but is hard to use on a real Monday with real students. I wanted to offer something more useful: honest guidance, practical strategies, and the kind of support I wish I had earlier when I first started teaching middle school.

I am not writing this from a distance. I still teach. I still live the realities of the classroom: the routines, the interruptions, the hard moments, the resets, and the small wins. This book is not theory from the sidelines. It comes from real classrooms, real students, and real experience.

This book is for teachers working with middle school students, early high school students, and especially ninth graders who are still adjusting to the structure and demands of secondary classrooms. It is for teachers who are tired of feeling like student behavior is setting the tone of the class. It is for teachers who want to lead with more clarity, more calm, and more confidence without becoming harsh, performative, or exhausted.

Everything in this book comes from experience—mistakes, reflection, trial and error, difficult days, small wins, and lessons learned in actual classrooms with actual students.

This is not a book about being the perfect teacher.

It is a book about building a classroom that works better.

A classroom with clearer expectations.

Stronger routines.

Better follow-through.

Less chaos.

Less emotional exhaustion.

And more of the kind of structure that makes learning possible.

If you are in your first years of teaching, or if classroom management still feels harder than it should, I wrote this for you.

Because struggling does not mean you are failing. Sometimes it means no one taught you the parts of teaching that become most important when the room is hard to lead.

This book is my attempt to offer that kind of help—clearly, honestly, and without wasting your time.

It begins with one shift that changed the way I saw classroom management:

The goal is not to control students.

The goal is to lead the room.

PART I:
BUILD THE FOUNDATION

Chapter 1
Lead the Room, Don't Try to Control It

When I first started teaching, I thought classroom management meant getting students under control. I thought it meant stopping the talking, correcting behavior, managing disruptions, and keeping the room from falling apart. I assumed most of the job was about reacting well.

That mindset caused more problems than I realized.

When classroom management feels like control, teachers often spend the day chasing behavior instead of building the conditions that make behavior better in the first place. The work becomes reactive, exhausting, and personal. Every interruption feels bigger. Every misstep feels like defiance. Every class starts to feel like something to survive.

But that is not the strongest way to think about classroom management.

The goal is not to control students.
The goal is to lead the room.

That shift matters because leadership changes what the teacher pays attention to. It moves the focus away from winning small power struggles and toward building a classroom with clear expectations, strong routines, calm correction, and consistent follow-through.

A well-led classroom does not happen because students are naturally compliant. It happens because the teacher creates enough clarity and structure for learning to function.

I remember a moment in my first year that taught me this lesson the hard way. I had a class that was struggling—not because the students were bad, but because I was spending all my energy reacting. Every side conversation became a confrontation. Every off-task moment felt personal. I was managing from frustration, not from a plan.

One afternoon, after a particularly exhausting period, I sat at my desk and realized I had spent more time correcting behavior than teaching content. That was the day I understood: I was not leading the room. I was chasing it.

The shift did not happen overnight. But once I started thinking more about structure than control, and more about systems than reactions, the room began to feel different. Not perfect, but more manageable. More intentional. More like a room I could actually lead.

This is true at every grade level, but it becomes especially clear in Grades 6–9. Students at this age often test limits, forget procedures, react emotionally, and struggle with consistency. Ninth grade can be especially challenging because students are older, but many still need the same clarity, repetition, and structure they resisted in earlier grades. Teachers sometimes expect high school students to arrive already knowing how to manage themselves well in class. Many do not.

That gap creates frustration. Teachers feel like students should know better. Students feel corrected all day without fully understanding what is expected. The classroom starts to run on reminders, redirection, and tension instead of systems that actually support behavior.

Leadership interrupts that cycle.

As Fred Jones explains in *Tools for Teaching*, the most effective teachers are not the ones constantly correcting behavior. They are the ones who have built a classroom where most correction becomes less necessary because the structure does so much of the heavy lifting. That shift—from reacting to leading—is where classroom management begins to work.

A teacher who leads the room does not wait for problems to grow before acting. That teacher teaches expectations clearly, builds routines on purpose, notices weak spots early, and responds with calm consistency.

Leadership is not about intimidation.
It is not about winning every confrontation.
It is not about having the loudest voice or the toughest attitude in the room.

It is about making the classroom feel structured, predictable, and clear.

Students do better when they know what happens here, what matters here, and what the teacher will do when something goes wrong. They may not always like the structure. They may still test it. But strong classroom management does not depend on students liking every expectation. It depends on the teacher being clear enough, steady enough, and consistent enough that the room does not drift into confusion.

That does not mean behavior problems disappear. They do not.
It does not mean every class becomes easy. It will not.

It does mean the teacher stops building the classroom around reaction and starts building it around leadership.

That is where classroom management becomes more effective.

It is also where teaching becomes less emotionally draining. When everything depends on reacting in the moment, the teacher is always one problem away from frustration. But when the room is built on routines, expectations, and follow-through, the teacher has something stronger than emotion to rely on. The classroom has a framework.

That framework will not solve everything, but it will solve more than teachers often realize.

Many teachers enter the profession believing that good intentions, engaging lessons, and strong relationships will be enough. Those things matter. But without leadership, they are not enough to hold the room together consistently.

Students need more than a kind teacher.
They need a clear teacher.
They need a steady teacher.
They need a teacher who can lead the room.

That is where this book begins.

Not with perfection.
Not with control.
With leadership.

What I Learned

Classroom management became more effective when I stopped thinking about it as control and started thinking about it as leadership.

Why This Works

When teachers focus on control, they often spend the day reacting to behavior. But when they focus on leadership, they pay more attention to structure, routines, expectations, and consistency. That shift helps the classroom feel calmer, clearer, and more predictable for both the teacher and the students.

Students do not need a teacher who reacts to every moment. They need a teacher who can set the tone, maintain structure, and lead the room with clarity.

Try This Tomorrow

Pay attention to one moment in your day when you feel yourself reacting instead of leading.

Ask yourself:

- Was the expectation clear?
- Was the routine strong?
- Did I respond from frustration or from structure?

Then choose one small way to lead the room more intentionally tomorrow. Maybe that means teaching a routine more clearly, correcting more calmly, or tightening a transition before it turns into chaos.

Do not try to fix everything at once. Start by seeing the work differently.

My Next Move

What is one area of my classroom where I need to stop reacting and start leading more intentionally?

____

____

____

____

If You Want to Go Deeper: *Fred Jones's Tools for Teaching offers one of the clearest explanations of why structure, presence, and calm consistency matter so much in classroom management. It is especially helpful for teachers who want to move away from constant correction and build a room that runs with more clarity.*

Chapter 2
Teach Expectation Before You Enforce Them

One of the biggest shifts I had to make as a teacher was understanding this: you cannot expect students to do what you have not clearly taught.

That sounds simple, but it changed everything for me.

At the beginning of my teaching career in middle school, I assumed too much. I assumed students knew what listening should look like. I assumed they knew how to enter the room, how to start class, how to ask for help, how to transition, how to work with a partner, and how to stay focused during instruction. I assumed that if I said something once, that was enough.

It was not.

Students need more clarity than we think. Every teacher runs a classroom differently. Every room has its own tone, routines, and limits. Even if students have heard a direction before, that does not mean they know what it looks like in your classroom. And even if they do, that does not mean they will do it consistently without reminders, modeling, and follow-through.

That is especially true in Grades 6–9.

At this age, students want independence, but they still need structure. They want to seem older, but many still need things broken down clearly. Ninth grade can be especially tricky because sometimes we expect students to act like fully mature high schoolers right away, when in reality many still need the same clarity, repetition, and structure they resisted the year before.

That is why one of the most useful things I learned was this: if I want a behavior, I need to teach it first.

As Harry Wong has said for decades, the number one problem in the classroom is not discipline. It is the lack of procedures and routines. Do not just mention it. Do not assume it. Teach it.

I also want to be clear about something that matters to me. I do not really use the word *rules* in my classroom. I use the word *expectations.*

That choice is intentional.

When I say *expectations*, I am not just giving students a list of things not to do. I am teaching them what needs to happen so the room can feel safe, respectful, and ready for learning. That language feels more aligned with the kind of classroom I want to build. It sounds less like control for the sake of control and more like guidance, clarity, and shared responsibility.

So instead of saying, "Here are my rules," I am really saying, "Here is what needs to happen in this room so learning can work."

That changes the tone. It also changes my mindset. Once I stopped thinking only in terms of rules, I became more focused on what I needed to teach, model, and reinforce.

One of the mistakes I made early on was treating expectations like a one-time conversation. I explained them at the beginning of the school year, and in my mind, that meant students should know them after that.

Over time, I learned that reteaching is part of teaching.

If the class gets off track, if routines start slipping, or if the room feels messy, I go back and reset.

That is not failure. That is good teaching.

That is why vague language does not help much.

"Be respectful" is too vague.
"Pay attention" is too vague.
"Act right" is too vague.

Students need to know what those things actually look like.

For me, that meant getting much more specific.

I taught students how to enter the classroom: enter calmly, go straight to your assigned seat, take out what you need, and begin the warm-up.

I taught them what respectful listening looked like: eyes on the speaker, body facing forward, no side conversations, no talking over someone else, and hands and feet to yourself.

I taught them how to ask for help: check your notes, check the directions, ask a classmate if appropriate, then ask me.

I taught them how to respond to an attention signal: stop, get quiet, and listen.

I taught them how to ask for the restroom or water, when it was appropriate, and what procedure to follow before leaving the room.

I taught them that seating mattered, movement mattered, timing mattered, and even small procedures mattered more than I had realized.

At first, I thought some of these things were too small to spend time on. But small procedures are not small when you are trying to teach through side conversations, confusion, wandering, repeated interruptions, and students constantly asking what they are supposed to be doing.

Those "small things" become big very quickly when they are not clear.

That is why I believe in teaching procedures as intentionally as I teach content.

Something else that helps, especially at this age, is using visuals. A simple visual can show students what you expect during entry, listening, transitions, group work, or asking for help. When I explain and model a procedure, it helps to have a visual they can look back at. That way, the expectation is not only said once. It stays visible.

If I want students to come in focused, I cannot just get annoyed when they enter loud and unprepared. I have to show them how I expect them to enter.

If I want students to listen while someone else is speaking, I cannot just say, "Stop talking." I have to teach what listening looks like.

If I want them to respond quickly when I need the room back, I have to teach the signal and the response that goes with it.

One thing that worked well in my classroom was using an attention signal that felt simple and memorable. I used a metal tone chime, which I called Dora.

When I rang Dora, students knew it meant voices off, eyes up, and bodies still. Because I did not compete with them, Dora never became background noise. It was the signal to stop, reset, and listen

But here is the part people skip: they did not automatically know that. I had to teach it, practice it with them, and correct it calmly until it became routine. Students this age still need repetition and structure, just delivered in a way that respects their age.

That is where humor helps.

Yes, even at this age.

I have used memes, funny slides, or small jokes tied to our classroom routines to build buy-in. A laugh lowers the tension, re-engages students, and gives their brains a quick reset so they can shift from social mode to learning mode more easily.

The goal is not to be a comedian. It is to use light, appropriate humor as a bridge—building connection first so students are more ready to respond.

That is what I mean by teaching an expectation. You do not just use the signal—you teach the response. Students need to know exactly what should happen when the chime rings, and then they need to practice it until it becomes routine. You reinforce it when they do it right, and you reteach it when they do not.

That principle shows up again and again in strong classroom management: procedures must be taught, not assumed.

Once I made that shift, I stopped misreading every problem.

I realized that not every behavior issue was defiance. Sometimes it was a lack of clarity. Sometimes students were doing what made sense to them because I had not clearly taught what I wanted instead. That does not mean students are never defiant. Sometimes they are. But I learned not to treat every problem like defiance when the real issue was that my expectation had not been taught, modeled, practiced, or reinforced enough.

That changed the way I responded.

Instead of only asking, "Why are they doing this?" I started asking, "Did I teach what I want clearly enough?"

That is a better question.

It keeps the teacher in a leadership mindset. It also helps prevent unnecessary frustration. Because if the issue is clarity, the answer is not more irritation. The answer is to clarify the expectation and reteach it.

And clearer expectations do not require a long speech.

They require modeling.
They require practice.
They require repetition.

Sometimes I modeled the procedure myself. Sometimes I asked a student to model it. Sometimes we practiced it more than once. Sometimes we reset and did it again because the first version was not good enough.

That can feel repetitive, especially when you are trying to get through a lesson. But I would rather spend time teaching a routine well than spend the rest of the week correcting the same preventable behavior over and over again.

The clearer you are on the front end, the less chaos you deal with later.

That is one of the most important things I want teachers to understand:

Teaching expectations is not wasting instructional time. It is protecting it.

And when students do meet expectations, that matters too.

I do not believe classroom management should sound only like correction. Students need to hear what they are doing well. They need reinforcement, not just redirection.

So when I see students doing the right thing, I say it.

"Thank you for getting started right away."
"I appreciate how quietly this side came in."
"That is what respectful listening looks like."
"Thank you for being ready."
"I like how you asked for help the right way."

That kind of language strengthens the behavior you want to keep seeing. It also helps create a classroom where students are not only hearing what they do wrong.

But reinforcement alone is not enough.

If expectations are taught but never enforced, students learn very quickly that the expectation is optional. You cannot teach one thing and accept another all the time.

Students notice that immediately.

That is why this work requires both clarity and follow-through.

I teach expectations. I model them. I practice them. I reinforce them. And I reteach them when needed.

I also think teachers need permission to reteach without embarrassment. Sometimes teachers feel like they should already be past that. They think, "By now they should know better." Maybe they should. But that thought does not fix the room.

Reteaching does.

If the entry routine is weak, reteach it.
If transitions are sloppy, reteach them.
If students are talking over instruction, reteach listening.
If the room feels off after a break, reset expectations.

That is not babying students. That is building a classroom where learning has a real chance to happen.

And honestly, this shift gave me a lot more peace. Not because my classroom became perfect. It did not. But it became clearer.
Calmer.
More predictable.
More teachable.

And that makes a huge difference.

What I Learned

I cannot hold students to expectations I have not clearly taught. The more specific I became about what I wanted, the more consistent my classroom became.

Why This Works

Students do better when expectations are visible, concrete, and practiced. When teachers teach procedures instead of assuming them, they reduce confusion, prevent avoidable behavior problems, and create a classroom that feels more predictable.

This also helps the teacher stay in a leadership mindset. Instead of reacting to every problem as defiance, the teacher can pause and ask whether the expectation was clearly taught, modeled, and reinforced.

Try This Tomorrow

Choose one routine or expectation that is not working as well as it should.

Ask yourself:

- Have I clearly taught what this should look like?
- Have I modeled it?
- Have students practiced it?
- Have I followed through consistently?

Then reteach that one expectation in a simple, concrete way. Do not give a long lecture. Show it, practice it, and reinforce it.

My Next Move

Which expectation in my classroom needs to be taught more clearly instead of repeated more loudly?

____

____

____

____

If You Want to Go Deeper: *Harry Wong's The First Days of School remains one of the most practical books on teaching procedures and expectations. It is especially useful for new teachers who want a step-by-step approach to building classroom structure.*

Chapter 3
Get the First Week Right

One of the biggest mistakes teachers make is treating the first week of school like a soft opening.

They wait to get serious later.
They assume routines can be built gradually.
They hope the class will settle into order naturally once everyone gets comfortable.

That is a costly mistake.

Because the first week does not just introduce the school year. It shows students what kind of classroom this is.

They are learning right away:

- how clear you are
- how consistent you are
- what you allow
- what you notice
- whether directions matter

- whether routines are real or optional

That is why the first week matters so much.

Harry Wong makes this point clearly: the first days of school set the tone for the year. Teachers who invest early in teaching procedures, rehearsing routines, and establishing clarity usually deal with fewer behavior problems later. Doug Lemov reinforces this with his idea of *Threshold*—the reminder that how a teacher manages the door, the greeting, and the first moments of class helps set the standard for everything else.

It is not because everything must be perfect.
It is because early patterns harden fast.

What feels small in the first week often becomes frustrating by the fifth week. If students enter loudly and aimlessly in August, that usually does not improve on its own by October. If transitions are messy from the beginning, that mess starts to feel normal. If the teacher repeats expectations without teaching them clearly, students stop hearing the words.

This is where many classroom management problems begin.

Not with extreme behavior.
With weak beginnings.

I learned that the hard way.

My first year, I spent most of the first week doing icebreakers, playing get-to-know-you games, and trying to be the teacher everyone liked. I barely mentioned procedures. I did not practice routines. I assumed structure would come naturally once students were comfortable.

By week three, the room was a mess.

Students entered however they wanted.
Transitions were chaotic.
Listening during instruction was a daily battle.

I spent the rest of the semester trying to build the structure I should have built from day one. It worked eventually, but it took far more energy than it would have if I had started with clarity.

The next year, I flipped it.

The first week was warm, but structured. I taught entry routines, practiced transitions, modeled listening expectations, and still built relationships—through the structure, not instead of it. We also practiced how to use materials from the classroom bookshelf, how to put them back correctly, and how to leave the space clean. I learned early on that if I did not teach that explicitly, I would end up doing the cleanup myself after every period.

That year started completely differently.

Early on, I thought being welcoming meant being loose. I thought I had time to tighten things later. In reality, the opposite was usually true. The longer I waited to clarify routines, the harder those routines were to establish. The more I let slide early, the more normal it became.

That is exhausting for teachers.
And confusing for students.

Because students adjust quickly to whatever the real system is.

Not the system written on your poster.
Not the system in your lesson plan.
The system you actually run.

If your real system is inconsistent, students learn inconsistency.
If your real system is unclear, students learn to guess.
If your real system changes with your mood, students learn to test it.

That is why the first week needs intention.

Teachers do not need to be harsh in the first week.
But they do need to be clear.

Some teachers hear "start strong" and think it means being overly strict, overly serious, or emotionally cold. I do not think that works well, especially in Grades 6–9. Students need warmth. They need to feel welcomed. They need to believe the room is safe and steady.

But warmth without structure creates problems.
And structure without warmth creates distance.

The goal is both.

Students should feel two things in the first week:

This teacher cares about us.
This teacher is going to run the room.

That combination builds trust much faster than either extreme.

So what should the first week actually do?

It should teach students how your classroom works.

That means the first week is not just about content. It is also about procedures, expectations, transitions, materials, attention signals, and what students should do when they are confused, entering the room, needing help, or working with others.

Teachers often underestimate how much students need things taught explicitly.

There is a difference between saying, "Be respectful," and teaching what respectful discussion sounds like. There is a difference between saying, "Come in quietly," and showing students exactly where to go, what to begin, and how quickly to do it. There is a difference between saying, "Pay attention," and teaching what attentive participation looks like in your room.

Students do better when the teacher makes the invisible visible.

Do not assume.
Show.
Do not just tell.
Model.
Then practice it until students can actually do it.

That may feel repetitive, but it saves time later. A teacher who spends ten minutes teaching and rehearsing a routine in August may save hours of correction by November.

That is a good trade.

I also think teachers get into trouble when they try to do too much too soon academically without securing the room first.

Of course instruction matters.
Of course the curriculum matters.

But if the room is disorganized, students do not yet know the systems, and basic procedures are shaky, the teacher ends up trying to teach content on top of confusion.

That usually creates more stress, not more rigor.

The stronger move is to use the first week to build the conditions that make instruction possible.

That means students should be learning content and learning the room at the same time. They should be practicing:

- how to enter
- how to begin class
- how to transition
- how to respond when you need attention
- how to use materials
- how to ask for help
- how to work with a partner
- how to end class

That is not extra.
That is classroom management at the most practical level.

Some teachers avoid this because they worry it feels too basic for older students. But even when students have done these things in another classroom, that does not mean they know how they work in yours. Every classroom has a different rhythm, a different standard, and a different teacher.

Students still need clarity.

That is especially true in Grades 6–9, where students move between multiple classes and multiple adults every day. If your room does not feel clear quickly, they bring their confusion, habits, and inconsistency right into it.

The first week also reveals a lot about teacher follow-through.

Students are watching closely at the beginning of the year. They notice whether you mean what you say. They notice whether directions actually matter. They notice whether you correct respectfully or inconsistently. They notice whether routines are practiced once and forgotten.

They are trying to understand the environment.
They want to know how this room works.

That is why follow-through matters so much during the first week.

If you say phones stay away, then phones need to stay away.
If you say voices should be off during directions, then you need to address side conversations.
If you teach an entry routine, then it has to matter every day, not only when you feel energetic enough to enforce it.

Students do not need perfection.
But they do need consistency strong enough to trust.

I also learned that the first week sets emotional tone as much as procedural tone.

Students need to feel that the room is calm, predictable, and led by an adult who is paying attention.

That does not come from long speeches.
It comes from repeated experiences.

They enter, and there is a clear start.
They get off track, and there is calm redirection.
They transition, and the teacher notices what is happening.
They meet expectations, and that gets named.

Those early experiences matter because they tell students whether the room is stable.

And stability is one of the strongest forms of classroom management.

I do not think the first week has to feel perfect to students. That is unrealistic.

Some routines will need to be retaught.
Some transitions will be awkward.
Some classes will feel stronger than others.

That is normal.

The point is not to perform perfection. The point is to notice quickly, adjust quickly, and keep teaching students how the room works.

That is what strong teachers do.

They do not panic every time something is messy.
They tighten it.
They reteach it.
They practice it again.

That is why the first week is not mainly about a teacher's energy.
It is about a teacher's clarity.

A very energetic teacher with weak systems can still have a chaotic room. A calm, clear teacher with solid routines often has a much easier year.

You do not need to entertain students into good behavior.
You do not need a perfect personality.
You do not need elaborate systems.

You need students to know what to do and believe that you will consistently lead them through it. That is what the first week should establish.

Because when the first week has structure, the rest of the year has something to stand on.

What I Learned

The first week of school is not a warm-up to the real year. It is the beginning of the real year. When I treated it casually, I spent months fixing preventable problems. When I used it to teach routines and set expectations clearly, the year felt much more manageable.

Why This Works

The first week sets patterns. Students quickly learn what matters, what gets enforced, and how the classroom actually runs. When teachers use those early days to teach procedures, practice routines, and follow through consistently, they create a classroom that feels clearer, calmer, and more predictable.

Strong beginnings do not eliminate every problem, but they prevent many unnecessary ones.

Try This Tomorrow

Think about the first ten minutes of class.

Ask yourself:

- Do students know exactly how to enter?
- Do they know what to do first without waiting on me?

- Have I taught that routine clearly enough to expect it consistently?

Then choose one part of your opening routine to tighten. Teach it, model it, practice it, and follow through on it.

Start with one routine. Make it clear. Make it real.

My Next Move

What is one routine I need to teach more clearly at the start of class so the rest of the period runs better?

____

____

____

____

If You Want to Go Deeper: *Harry Wong's The First Days of School and Doug Lemov's Teach Like a Champion both offer practical strategies for making the opening of the year count. If you can read only one section of either book before school starts, focus on the parts about procedures, routines, and how to begin class with clarity.*

Chapter 4
Build Routines That Run the Classroom

One of the most practical things I learned about classroom management is this: students do better when class feels predictable.

Honestly, most people do.

When students know how class starts, where they sit, what they should do first, how they ask for help, and what happens next, there is less confusion, less wasted time, and less room for unnecessary behavior problems to grow.

That changed a lot for me.

As Doug Lemov explains in Teach Like a Champion, a strong, structured start sets the tone for everything that follows. When the beginning of class is clear and consistent, the teacher starts from a position of leadership instead of spending the first few minutes trying to settle the room.

At first, I thought classroom management was mostly about correcting behavior after it happened. I thought I needed to respond better in the moment, be firmer, and stay on top of disruptions. Some of that mattered. But over time, I realized something else mattered just as much: a lot of my frustration was coming from things that were too unclear.

Students were not always trying to challenge me.

Sometimes they were filling in the gaps.

If the beginning of class was loose, they filled it with talking.

If transitions were unclear, they filled them with noise.

If early finishers had nothing to do, they filled the time with distraction.

If asking for help was not structured, they filled the room with interruptions.

That is when I started understanding the power of routines.

Not complicated routines.

Clear ones.

A strong classroom does not run on constant correction. It runs on systems students can follow every day without having to guess what happens next.

If the room feels too loose, too inconsistent, or too unclear, students will show you quickly.

That is why routines matter.

They reduce guessing.
They reduce dead time.
They reduce unnecessary decisions.
And they reduce how often the teacher has to manage preventable problems in real time.

One of the first routines that helped my classroom run better was making sure students had something to do as soon as they walked in.

If students enter the room and have nothing to begin, those first few minutes disappear quickly. Students start talking, wandering, delaying, or waiting for the teacher to settle the room before class actually begins.

I saw this clearly during my first year. For the first two weeks, my classes had no bellringer routine and no assigned seats. Students drifted in, sat wherever they wanted, and started socializing. By the time I tried to begin instruction, I had already lost them. The energy in the room was theirs, not mine.

When I introduced a consistent warm-up and assigned seats, the difference was immediate. Students still talked, but they had something in front of them. They knew what to do. And I had a little space to take attendance and breathe instead of begging the room to settle down.

That small change saved me more energy than I expected. That is why I like starting class with a consistent warm-up. It gives students an immediate job. They come in, go to their assigned seat, get their materials out, and begin. Even on days when I do something different, students still ask about the warm-up because it has become part of how they enter the room.

I also use a timer. Usually, I give students four or five minutes and keep the timer visible so they know how much time they have before we review it together. That matters more than it may seem. If the warm-up drags on too long, students finish early, lose focus, and the room starts to slip. A warm-up should be short enough to get students thinking, not long enough to create dead time.

The warm-up does not need to be elaborate. It should be brief, focused, and connected to the learning. Most days, I use it to review something we are already working on, activate prior knowledge, or prepare students for the lesson ahead.

It can be:

- one review question
- a short writing prompt
- vocabulary or skill practice
- a simple do-now connected to the previous lesson

The goal is not to impress students.

The goal is to make the beginning of class predictable.

But a warm-up only helps if students know exactly what entering class should look like.

I cannot just say, "Do your warm-up," if I have never taught what entering class means in my room.

I need to be specific:

When you enter class, go straight to your assigned seat, take out what you need, and begin the warm-up quietly.

That is much clearer than, "Okay, get started."

Students need direct instructions, especially when a routine is still being built. At the beginning of the year, after breaks, or anytime the routine starts to slip, I go back and reteach it.

Assigned seats also helped my classroom more than I expected.

I know some teachers resist them because they want students to choose responsibly. I understand that. But in real classrooms, students do not always make the best choices about where they sit. They sit near friends. They sit near the person who distracts them most. They pick the place where they know they can get away with more.

Then the teacher spends energy managing problems that are easier to prevent than to fix.

Assigned seats help with:

- reducing side conversations
- separating students who feed off each other
- learning names faster
- settling students more quickly
- simplifying group work

Assigned seats do not fix everything, but they remove a lot of unnecessary friction.

Sometimes structure is support.

Another routine that mattered was teaching what listening during instruction actually looked like.

At first, I assumed students understood what "listen" meant. But that word is too vague if the teacher has never made it visible. I had to define it in concrete, observable ways. Students needed to know what listening looked like during directions, what was not acceptable while someone else was speaking, and how quickly I expected them to reset when I needed the room back.

That kind of clarity helped.

So did changing my own response.

One of the most practical lessons I learned was this: if students started talking while I was talking, the worst thing I could do was keep talking over them.

That only trained them not to listen the first time. It also raised the noise in the room and made the moment more chaotic.

So I stopped doing that.

If students talked, I stopped talking.

I waited.

Most of the time, they quieted down. If they did not, I redirected the group calmly without turning it into a public battle. I might say, "I'm waiting on this side of the room," or, "I need everyone with me." Then, when they settled, I thanked them and moved on.

That is why routines matter so much. Classroom management is rarely built through one dramatic intervention. It is built through repeated, predictable responses to everyday moments.

Another routine that helped was deciding ahead of time how I would check for understanding.

Without a routine for that, confusion can sit in the room too long. Then students get lost, stop trying, start talking, or become dependent on the teacher repeating everything individually.

So I needed simple ways to check whether students were actually with me.

That could look like:

- a thumbs up or thumbs down
- one problem on a whiteboard
- a short turn-and-talk
- a quick written response
- an exit ticket
- a short digital check-in

The point is not the format. The point is that checking for understanding became part of the structure of class.

I also had to teach students how to ask for help.

That is one of those things teachers sometimes overlook because it seems obvious. But if students do not know the procedure, they will create one on their own.

They will call out.

Leave their seat.

Interrupt instruction.

Wait too long.

Or shut down completely.

That is why a help routine matters.

Students need to know:

- Do they raise a hand?
- Do they check directions first?
- Can they ask a partner?

- What if I am already helping someone else?
- What do they do while they wait?

The same thing is true for early finishers. If students finish early and there is no routine, "I'm done" quickly becomes talking, wandering, or bothering other students.

So early finishers need a plan too.

That might be:

- reading quietly
- continuing unfinished work
- a short extension task
- vocabulary review
- an extra prompt

The exact activity matters less than the fact that students already know there is one.

Transitions were another huge area.

A lot of behavior problems do not happen during instruction itself. They happen between parts of the lesson. The mini-lesson may go fine. Then it is time to move into groups, get materials, switch tasks, or clean up, and suddenly the room gets loud, messy, and slow.

That is why transitions need routines too.

If I say, "Get into groups," and that is the full direction, I may get ten different versions of what students think that means.

The more specific I am, the smoother the transition becomes.

One tool that helped me make transitions and activities clearer was CHAMPS. I know some people think CHAMPS is only for elementary classrooms, but I do not see it that way. Students in Grades 6–9 need visible expectations too.

What helped was not making the system complicated. I did not need students to memorize an abstract acronym. I needed to make expectations visible. When we moved from the warm-up to independent work, partner work, or small groups, students needed to know the CHAMPS for that moment:

- What is the conversation level?
- How do we get help?
- What is the activity?
- Can we move?
- What does participation look like?

That made transitions smoother and gave students fewer chances to guess wrong.

Sometimes the easiest way to do that was with a CHAMPS-style poster and movable magnets. Before the activity started, I could quickly show the voice level, whether the task was independent or with a partner, what movement was allowed, and how students should get help.

It took less than a minute, but it prevented a lot of confusion.

CHAMPS did not replace routines.
It supported them.

Another important thing I had to learn is that a well-managed classroom is not always a silent classroom.

I believe in collaborative work. Students need chances to talk, move, exchange ideas, and process learning with other people. Especially in Grades 6–9, it is not realistic to expect students to sit still for 45 or 50 minutes without moving or speaking. Honestly, even as an adult, I would struggle with that. So I cannot expect it from them all day either.

That is why I try to build lessons that shift intentionally. There are moments for direct instruction, moments for quiet work, and moments when students need to get up, talk to a partner, analyze something together, or move through a more active task. That is not a break from classroom management.

That is classroom management.

Sometimes teachers think management means students sitting silently the entire period. I do not see it that way. A classroom can be active and still be well run. Students can be talking and still be on task. Movement is not the problem. Talking is not the problem. The problem is when those things happen without structure, without expectations, and without follow-through.

That is why I decide ahead of time what kind of activity we are doing and what I want the room to sound like during that time. If students are working with a partner or in a group, I need to be clear about the voice level, movement, participation, and how they get help.

When students sit too long without movement, many of them start looking for stimulation somewhere else. That may show up as talking, getting out of their seats, distracting others, or simply checking out. That is not always defiance. Sometimes it is restlessness, boredom, or the simple fact that the lesson has asked for too much stillness for too long.

That is especially true during parts of class that are more teacher-directed or more abstract. Not every part of a lesson will feel exciting to students, and that is just real teaching. Sometimes we do have to teach content that feels heavier or is simply harder for students to stay engaged with. But that is also a reminder that the classroom cannot stay teacher-centered all the time. Students need chances to think, talk, process, and do something with what they are learning. When too much of the lesson depends on students sitting and receiving for long stretches, attention starts to fade.

If I know a section of the lesson is going to be heavier, then I need to think ahead. A structured turn-and-talk, a quick movement task, a partner discussion, a brief collaborative task, or a short reset can help students re-engage before off-task behavior starts taking over. Sometimes better classroom management is not about more correction. Sometimes it is about shifting the lesson so students are carrying more of the thinking and more of the learning.

In that sense, movement is not a distraction from classroom management.

Used well, it is part of classroom management.

It helps students stay engaged, helps prevent avoidable behavior problems, and gives the teacher a more realistic way to lead the room.

The goal is not a silent room all day.

The goal is a room that can shift when needed.

A room that can handle quiet.

A room that can handle collaboration.

A room that can handle movement without falling apart.

That kind of flexibility is part of strong classroom management too.

And when transitions are weak, I should not just get frustrated. I should reteach them.

We practice how to move into groups.
We practice how to get materials.
We practice how to clean up and reset.

That is not wasted time.
That is classroom management.

I learned that when routines start to slip, I always have two choices: keep repeating the same correction or stop and reteach the routine. Reteaching works better.

If the entry routine gets messy, I review it.
If the warm-up gets weaker, I reset it.
If students are interrupting instruction, I go back to the listening expectation.
If transitions get sloppy, we practice them again.

A lot of teachers get frustrated because they think students should already know better by then. Sometimes they probably should. But that thought does not fix the room.
Reteaching does.

That is one of the biggest reasons routines matter so much. They reduce the number of decisions students have to make in the moment, and they reduce the number the teacher has to make too.

This is how we enter.
This is how we begin.
This is how you get help.

This is what you do when you finish.
This is how we move from one part of class to the next.

That kind of clarity strengthens the room.

Teachers like Harry Wong have emphasized for years that procedures matter, and honestly, this is one place where that advice holds up in real classrooms. The difference is that routines only help if the teacher actually teaches them, practices them, and revisits them when they start to slip.

That is the part that matters most.

What helped my classroom run better was not one magic strategy. It was building routines strong enough that the room did not have to depend on my frustration, my volume, or my constant improvisation.

That made the classroom better for students.

And it made teaching more sustainable for me.

What I Learned

My classroom got better when I stopped relying on correction alone and started building routines students could follow every day. The more predictable class became, the less energy I had to spend managing preventable problems in the moment.

Why This Works

Routines reduce confusion, wasted time, and unnecessary decision-making. They make expectations visible and give students a structure they can follow without guessing. That helps the room feel calmer and helps the teacher lead with more consistency.

Strong routines also make reteaching easier. When something slips, the teacher has something clear to return to.

Try This Tomorrow

Choose one part of your class that regularly feels messy.

Ask yourself:

- Have I taught a clear routine for this?
- Do students know exactly what it should look like?
- Have I practiced it enough to expect it consistently?

Then tighten that one routine. Teach it clearly, model it, and practice it again.

Do not try to fix the whole room at once.

Build one strong routine at a time.

Reflect and Reset

When part of the day keeps falling apart, do I keep reacting to it, or do I stop and ask whether the routine is solid enough to hold?

My Next Move

What is one routine in my classroom that needs to be tightened, retaught, or followed more consistently?

____

____

____

____

If You Want to Go Deeper: *Harry Wong's The First Days of School remains one of the most practical resources for understanding why routines and procedures matter so much. It is especially useful for teachers who want to build a classroom that feels more predictable, organized, and manageable from the very beginning.*

Chapter 5
Give Students a Role in the Room

One classroom management strategy that has helped me more than I expected is giving students classroom jobs.

I know that for some teachers, classroom jobs sound like something that belongs in elementary school. They may picture something too young, too cute, or too disconnected from what middle and high school students actually need. But that has not been my experience.

In my classroom, jobs are not there just to fill a chart. They are part of how the room functions.

They build responsibility.
They build ownership.
They help students feel like they belong in the room.

And honestly, they help me too.

That matters, because a classroom runs better when the teacher is not trying to carry every small responsibility alone.

At some point, I started asking myself a practical question:

What does my classroom actually need in order to run well?

Not what looks cute.
Not what would look nice on a bulletin board.
What does the room really need?

That question changed how I thought about classroom jobs.

Once I stopped seeing them as something extra, I started seeing them as part of the structure of the classroom. If I need help remembering attendance, that can become a job. If I need the board erased before the next class comes in, that can become a job. If I need materials passed out quickly, pencils returned correctly, Chromebooks checked, trash picked up, or desks straightened, those can all become jobs too.

That is how I use them.

For example, I am the kind of teacher who can forget to take attendance.

Not once in a while.
Constantly.

So I have an Attendance Helper in every class period. That student writes the absences on the board for me, and then I can officially record them during a natural break in class or during the passing period.

That may sound small, but it helps me a lot. It is one less thing I have to hold in my head while I am also trying to teach.

The same is true with my Board Eraser. There have been plenty of times when I forgot to erase the warm-up answers from the previous class, and the next group walked in with the answers already on the board.

That is not how I want to start class.

So having a student responsible for erasing the board and clearing the attendance list during the last few minutes of class helps the next period begin better.

I also use jobs like Material Passer, Material Collector, Desk Organizer, Trash Patrol, Bookshelf Organizer, Teacher Helper, and others that simply help the room run more smoothly.

Material Passers and Material Collectors help transitions move faster.
Desk Organizer helps keep the room orderly.
Trash Patrol helps keep the classroom clean at the end of class.
Bookshelf Organizer keeps that area from slowly becoming messy and ignored.

Those jobs may seem small, but they matter.

In fact, the custodians have told me more than once, "Miss, your classroom is one of the cleanest at the end of the day."

And honestly, that is not because of me alone.

That is because my students help take care of the room.

I remind them often that this classroom is their second home during the school day. If we spend that much time here, we should take care of it together.

That message matters.

It builds ownership.
It builds responsibility.
And it helps students understand that the classroom is not just a place they pass through. It is a place they help maintain.

That sense of belonging can help behavior more than people think.

Students often do better when they feel like they are part of the room, not just people sitting in it waiting to be corrected. They respond differently when they are trusted with something. They respond differently when they feel useful. They respond differently when they know they have a role.

That is especially true in Grades 6–9.

Students at this age want to feel capable.
They want some independence.
They want to know they matter.

Many of them respond well when responsibility is built into the room in a real, visible way.

I have seen this help especially with students who are restless or need movement. Some students do better when they have a job that gives them a reason to move with purpose instead of finding reasons to move at the wrong time.

That is why jobs like Door Holder, Board Eraser, Materials Helper, or other movement-based roles can be so useful. For some students, movement is going to happen one way or another. I would rather give it structure than spend the whole period correcting random wandering.

That does not mean every student who needs movement will suddenly become easy to manage. It does not mean a classroom job replaces clear expectations, consequences, or follow-through.

But it can help.

Sometimes the right responsibility reduces the wrong behavior.

Other jobs support students in quieter ways. A Tutor can help classmates with translations, directions, missed work, or reviewing assignments before they submit them. An On-Call student can fill in when someone is absent. A Pencils Helper can make sure every student returns the numbered pencil that matches their seat number. A Chromebook Helper can check that all devices are accounted for and organized on Chromebook days. A Bathroom or Water Helper can help keep sign-outs and returns clear.

Again, none of this is random.

These jobs exist because they support what the room needs.

That is one of the most important things I want teachers to understand: classroom jobs should make sense for your classroom.

You do not need to copy someone else's list exactly.
You do not need to create jobs just to say you have them.
You need to think about the real needs of your room.

What do you keep forgetting?
What keeps interrupting your flow?
What small responsibilities pull your attention away from instruction?
What routines could students help maintain?
What kind of movement could become more purposeful?
What would help the room function better every day?

That is where your jobs should come from.

Another part that matters to me is how students get those jobs. I do not like assigning them with no student voice at all. I want students to have some ownership in the process.

So one strategy I use is a gallery walk. I post the classroom jobs and their descriptions around the room, and students walk around reading them. They think about which jobs fit them best. Then they write down their top choices.

Usually, I ask students for their top three or four choices. I also ask them to list other jobs they think they could do well and explain why they would be a good fit. I ask them to tell me which jobs would not be a good fit too. That gives me useful information. It helps me avoid placing students in roles they do not want or are not ready to handle, because the goal is for them to help and feel useful, not to force them into something that does not fit.

That part matters.
It gives students a voice.
It helps me understand how they see themselves.
And it gives me better information if I cannot give them one of their top choices.

Because classroom jobs are not just little rewards.
They are responsibilities.
And I present them that way.

I tell students that these jobs help the classroom flow and that everyone contributes to making the room work. The goal is not to hand out titles just to make students feel important. The goal is to help the classroom run better for everyone.

That changes the tone.

I also rotate jobs every marking period.

That gives students another opportunity.

It keeps the system from getting stale.

And it gives me room to adjust based on what I have learned.

In some classes, I may have more students than I have jobs. When that happens, I still try to make sure every student has a role. Sometimes that means assigning two or three students to the same job. Sometimes it means giving a student an on-call role so they can step in when someone is absent or when I need extra help. That flexibility matters. It keeps the system inclusive, and it keeps the classroom from depending too much on one student being there every day.

Sometimes a student is ready for more responsibility later. Sometimes a student who struggled in one role may do better in another. Sometimes a student's strengths become clearer once I know them better.

Another thing that helps is giving students some kind of recognition for doing their jobs well.

In my school, we use something called Bucks. Students earn them for being responsible, respectful, and kind. For me, doing your classroom job consistently is part of being responsible, so when students handled their jobs well, I often gave them Bucks as a kind of pay.

That worked well in my classroom.

Students could save them and use them later in the school store for prizes, snacks, or small rewards. It gave the system a little more weight and helped students take their responsibilities seriously. And honestly, they liked feeling like their effort was being noticed.

I do not think every classroom job system has to include tangible rewards. Some teachers use jobs without giving anything physical, and that can absolutely work too. Sometimes the responsibility itself, the ownership, and the trust are enough. Other times, a small privilege can work just as well.

The key is that whatever students earn should feel structured and earned, not random.

And if your school does not use something like Bucks, that does not mean you cannot make the system work. You can use a simple point system, small privileges, or no reward at all if the responsibility itself is enough.

If rewards are something you want to offer but do not have the budget for, families can often help more than teachers expect. A short note in a class newsletter or an Amazon wish list can make it easier to gather small items that support the classroom.

But I want to say this clearly: if you do not have rewards, do not let that stop you from trying classroom jobs.

The point of the system is bigger than prizes.

The point is responsibility.
The point is ownership.
The point is belonging.

Rewards can support that.
They are not the reason the system works.

What matters most is that students understand their role matters and that helping the classroom run well is something worth taking seriously.

Classroom jobs are one of those strategies that support both structure and connection at the same time. They help the room feel more organized. They help students feel more involved. They help the teacher carry less alone. And in many cases, they reduce small problems before those problems start pulling too much attention away from instruction.

That is what makes them worth it to me.

This is not about creating a perfect system. It is about asking:

What would help my room run better?
What can students help carry?
How can responsibility become part of the structure of my classroom?

Those are good questions.

And for me, classroom jobs have been one strong answer.

What I Learned

Classroom jobs helped my room run better when I stopped thinking of them as something extra and started seeing them as part of the structure. They gave students responsibility, gave the classroom more order, and helped me carry less by myself.

Why This Works

Students often do better when they feel useful, trusted, and connected to the room. Classroom jobs give them a clear role and make responsibility visible. They also help the teacher protect time and energy by sharing small tasks that can otherwise interrupt instruction.

When jobs are practical and purposeful, they strengthen both structure and belonging.

Try This Tomorrow

Think about one small responsibility in your classroom that keeps interrupting your flow.

Ask yourself:

- Could a student help with this consistently?
- Would turning this into a job help the room run better?
- Which student might benefit from that responsibility?

Then create one simple classroom job based on a real need in your room. Explain it clearly, give it purpose, and treat it like a real responsibility.

Start small.
Make it useful.
See what changes.

My Next Move

What is one classroom job or student responsibility I can create this week that would help my classroom run better?

____

____

____

____

If You Want to Go Deeper: *Michael Linsin's The Classroom Management Secret offers practical ideas for building responsibility, clarity, and smoother classroom systems without overcomplicating them. It is especially helpful for teachers who want students to take more ownership in how the room functions.*

Chapter 6
Build Connection Before You Correct

One of the biggest mindset shifts I had to make as a teacher was understanding that classroom management is not just about control.

It is also about connection.

That does not mean being permissive.
It does not mean letting students do whatever they want.
And it definitely does not mean trying to be their friend.

It means understanding that students respond better when they feel seen, respected, and safe in your classroom.

Students at this age often act like they do not care, but they care about everything. They care about how they look, how their peers see them, whether they feel embarrassed, whether they feel singled out, and whether the adult in the room genuinely likes them.

They may never say that out loud.
But you can see it in how they respond.

That is why connection matters so much.

As Ross Greene writes in *Lost at School*, "Kids do well if they can." That idea has shaped a lot of how I think about classroom management. If a student is struggling, the first question should not always be, *What consequence fits?* Sometimes it should be, *What is getting in the way?*

Connection gives you a better chance of answering that question honestly.

I learned that students are much more likely to accept correction from a teacher who has already built some kind of relationship with them. If all they ever hear from you is correction, redirection, and consequences, eventually they stop hearing your voice as support.

They only hear control.

And once that happens, everything gets harder.

That does not mean connection fixes everything.

It does not.

You still need expectations.
You still need routines.
You still need follow-through.

But connection changes the way those things land.

For me, connection started with small things:

- greeting students at the door
- learning their names quickly
- smiling at them
- checking in

- noticing when something felt off
- asking questions that had nothing to do with academics

Sometimes connection looked like humor.

I do not mean trying to be funny all the time. I mean those small, natural moments that make the room feel human—a quick comment, a light observation, something that helps students relax for a second. Students often come into class with their guard up. A little laughter can lower that guard and make the room feel safer.

Sometimes connection looked like simple interest.

At the beginning of the year, I liked using a student questionnaire and asking about favorite candy, favorite sport, favorite show, or favorite music. That may sound small, but those details matter. Students notice when you remember something about them. They notice when you ask how their weekend went. They notice when you remember they had a game or bring up something they care about.

That kind of thing builds trust.

And trust matters in classroom management more than people think.

When students trust that you are not trying to embarrass them, they are less likely to fight you on everything. When they feel safe with you, they are more open to redirection. When they feel like your classroom is a place where they belong, they are more willing to participate, take risks, and recover from mistakes.

I also learned that connection shows up in how you correct students.

One thing I believe strongly is this:

Praise in public.
Correct in private.

If a student needs redirection, I do not want to embarrass them in front of everyone else if I can avoid it. I do not want correction to become a performance. So if I can, I pull them aside. I lower my voice. I talk to them after class. I try to keep their dignity intact.

That matters more than people realize.

A student who feels humiliated will often shut down, act out more, or become defensive. A student who feels respected is much more likely to actually hear what you are saying.

One experience that stayed with me involved a student I will call Pete. He was struggling in my class. Pete was often late, missing work, and needed repeated redirection. I was frustrated with him, and one of the things I kept correcting was that he always wore his hoodie in class.

After I contacted home about his grades and behavior, another teacher did too. In response, his mother shaved his head as a punishment. The next time Pete came into class, he was wearing the hoodie again. I was ready to address it. But before I could, he looked at me quietly and said, "Miss, please. I'm begging you. Please let me keep my hoodie on."

Then he showed me why.

Under the hoodie, his head had been shaved.

In that moment, my frustration disappeared.

What I had been seeing was still real. He was failing, late, and off task. But now I saw something else too. I saw embarrassment. I saw shame. I saw a student trying to protect himself. At that age, appearance matters so much, and in that moment I realized he was not just resisting an expectation.

He was trying not to feel exposed.

That moment stayed with me because it reminded me of something important:

Behavior is not always the whole story.

Sometimes what looks like defiance is pain.
Sometimes what looks like laziness is heaviness.
Sometimes what looks like not caring is hurt.

That does not mean we stop holding students accountable.

It means we pause before assuming we know the whole story.

That is one reason connection matters. It helps us respond with more understanding, not just more reaction.

And I think that matters a lot in Grades 6–9.

Students this age are impulsive, emotional, peer-conscious, and often carrying more than adults realize. Some are loud about it. Some are not. Some test you constantly. Some avoid eye contact. Some laugh when they are uncomfortable. Some come in with walls already up.

Those are often the students who need the most consistency, the most calm, and the most care.

That does not mean lowering your standards for them.

It means not giving up on them just because they do not respond right away.

Connection takes time.

Sometimes it looks like a conversation.
Sometimes it looks like noticing.
Sometimes it looks like greeting a student every day even when they

barely respond.
Sometimes it looks like praising a small improvement that other people would miss.

Those small things add up.

At the same time, I want to say this clearly: a good relationship with students does not mean they always feel good about you.

Sometimes students are frustrated with the teacher who holds them accountable. Sometimes they like the teacher who lets more slide. Sometimes they need a boundary they do not appreciate in the moment.

That is part of the job.

If your definition of a good relationship is that students are never upset with you, your classroom management will get weak fast.

Because part of being the adult is being willing to disappoint students sometimes.

Not unfairly.
Not harshly.
Not unnecessarily.
But clearly.

That is part of leadership.

This is where many teachers get confused. They work hard to build relationships and then feel discouraged when behavior problems still happen.

But connection and structure are not the same thing.

You need both.

Relationships help classroom management, but they do not replace expectations, routines, consistency, boundaries, or consequences.

A strong relationship does not mean a student gets whatever they want from you.
It does not mean there are no boundaries.
It does not mean you never say no.

In fact, I think relationships are often stronger when students know the teacher is both caring and firm.

Students need warmth, yes.
But they also need steadiness.
They need clarity.
They need adults who mean what they say.

My students know I care about them. I joke with them. I listen to them. I show up for them. But they also know not to cross the line. When I teach an expectation, I follow through. I do not yell, and I do not give ten warnings. I give one warning, and then I act.

They know that if they choose not to follow expectations, I will still follow through with the consequence.

That is the balance I want in my classroom.

It is not love or structure.
It is love with structure.

And I think students feel that.

I also think relationships are stronger when students can trust your fairness, not just your friendliness.

Students pay attention to whether you are consistent. They notice whether you embarrass people. They notice whether you listen before reacting. They notice whether expectations apply to everyone. They notice whether your mood changes the rules.

All of that shapes relationships.

That is why I think some teachers misunderstand what students really mean when they say they like a teacher.

Sometimes they do mean the teacher is funny or nice.

But often they also mean:

- this teacher is fair
- this teacher respects us
- this teacher is genuine
- this teacher does not humiliate people
- this teacher listens
- this teacher actually cares
- this teacher means what they say

That is deeper than just being liked.

If I had to say it simply, I would say this: students should know that I care about them, but they should also know that caring about them does not mean I will lower every standard, ignore every behavior, or stop leading the room.

Real care does not remove accountability.
Sometimes it requires it.

A classroom where students feel seen but not led can become chaotic.

A classroom where students feel managed but not seen can become cold.

Neither one is the goal.

The goal is both.
A room where students feel respected and guided.
A room where they feel known and accountable.
A room where warmth and structure work together.

That kind of classroom is powerful.
And it starts with connection.

What I Learned

Students respond better to correction when they feel respected, safe, and seen, not just treated as behavior problems. Connection did not replace expectations in my classroom, but it made those expectations easier for students to hear and easier for me to enforce calmly.

Why This Works

Connection builds trust, and trust changes how correction is received. When students feel respected and emotionally safe, they are less likely to become defensive and more likely to respond to redirection. At the same time, connection works best when it is paired with clear boundaries and steady follow-through.

Warmth helps students feel safe.
Structure helps students stay safe.

Students need both.

Try This Tomorrow

Choose one student who has been harder for you to reach.

Ask yourself:

- What do I know about this student besides the behavior?
- Have I had any interaction with this student that was not correction?
- Is there one small way I can build trust before the next redirection?

Then do one small thing: greet them by name, ask a genuine question, notice an effort, or correct them more privately and calmly than usual.

Do not force a big moment.

Start with one small act of connection.

My Next Move

Which student in my classroom needs more connection from me before my correction will truly land?

____

____

____

____

If You Want to Go Deeper: *Ross Greene's Lost at School offers a compelling framework for understanding student behavior through a lens of skill deficits rather than willful defiance. It is especially useful for teachers who work with students whose behavior feels confusing or resistant to traditional approaches.*

PART II:
DAILY CLASSROOM MANAGEMENT

Chapter 7
Follow Through Every Time

One of the fastest ways to weaken classroom management is to say something and then not follow through.

I learned that the hard way.

In my first year of teaching middle school, there were times when I gave a warning, named a consequence, or told a student what would happen next, but when the moment came, I hesitated. Sometimes I repeated myself too much. Sometimes I negotiated. Sometimes I let it go because I was tired, because I did not want to escalate the situation, or because I hoped the student would make a better choice on their own. If I am honest, there were also times when I delayed the next step because contacting home took time, required explanation, and sometimes felt like more emotional labor than I had the capacity for in that moment.

Students notice that quickly.

They notice when you do not mean what you say.
They notice when consequences are only words.
And once they notice that, they start testing more.

That does not always mean they are bad kids. Often, it means they are trying to figure out whether your boundaries are real.

A classroom can have clear expectations, strong routines, and solid structure. But if students learn that the teacher does not consistently follow through, all of that starts to weaken. The room becomes more negotiable. Directions start sounding optional. Warnings lose value. The teacher ends up repeating the same things over and over, getting more frustrated each time.

That cycle is exhausting.

And honestly, it can make teachers feel weaker than they really are.

Because the issue is not always that the teacher lacks authority. Sometimes the issue is that the teacher is not consistently using the authority they already have.

Follow-through does not mean being harsh, turning every moment into punishment, escalating too quickly, or acting cold. It means that when I say something will happen, I do it.

If I say students need to stop talking, then I cannot keep teaching over the talking and pretend I enforced it. If I say a student will move seats after a warning, then I need to move the seat if the behavior continues. If I say I will contact home, then I need to contact home. If I say a consequence will happen next, then that consequence needs to happen.

Otherwise, my words start losing weight.

That is why follow-through matters so much. Students do not need big speeches without action. They need a teacher whose words mean something.

And I want to say this clearly: follow-through does not require a big performance. In fact, it usually works better when it is calm. The stronger teacher response is often the shorter one.

This is your warning.
I already redirected this.
Now you need to move.
I said I would call home, so I am calling home.
That is the consequence.

That kind of language is simple, but it carries weight because it is clear and final.

No speech.
No emotional spiral.
No long argument.
No need to prove how serious you are with volume.

Just clarity, action, and follow-through.

As Lee Canter's work on assertive discipline makes clear, effective teachers are neither passive nor hostile. They are assertive—clear about expectations, confident in follow-through, and calm in delivery. The power is not in the volume. It is in the certainty.

One of the biggest mistakes I made early on was giving too many warnings.

I understand why teachers do this. Sometimes we want to give students another chance. Sometimes we are trying to avoid conflict. Sometimes we are just tired and do not want to deal with the next step.

But too many warnings teach the wrong lesson.

I learned this the hard way with a student I will call Marcus. He was a seventh grader who tested boundaries constantly, but never in a way that felt extreme, just persistent. He would talk during instruction, get out of his seat, tap on the desk, and whisper to friends. Every day, I gave him three or four warnings before doing anything. And every day, he learned exactly how far he could go before I acted.

One afternoon, after the fifth warning, another student said out loud, "Miss, you always say that, but you never do anything." A few students laughed, and I felt my face get hot.

That comment stung.

But it was honest.

The next day, I told Marcus his first warning would be his only warning. If the behavior continued, I would move his seat.

No negotiation.

When it happened, I moved him.

He was surprised.
He complained.
He asked for another chance.

I told him he had already had his chance, and I moved him.

Then the room got quieter.

Not because I was harsh.
Because I finally meant what I said.

Too many warnings teach students that the first warning does not matter. Then the second one does not matter. Then the third one barely matters. By the time the teacher finally acts, students have already learned that action takes too long.

That makes behavior worse, not better.

Now, I am not saying every behavior needs an immediate consequence with no room for judgment. Teachers need judgment. Context matters. Some students need redirection more than punishment. Some moments need flexibility. Some situations are minor and can be handled quickly and quietly.

But if I set a boundary, I need to mean it.

That is the difference.

Students can handle firmness better than inconsistency. They may not like consequences. They may complain. They may test. But many students actually feel more secure when the adult in the room stays calm and follows through.

This matters especially with students who push back. When a student challenges a boundary, it can be tempting to talk too much. We explain, warn again, debate, repeat ourselves, and try to convince them to make the right choice. But in many cases, that only turns the moment into a power struggle.

And power struggles usually make things worse.

The more the teacher talks, the more room there is for the student to push back, perform for peers, or drag the moment out.

That is why follow-through often needs to be brief.

State the expectation.
Give the direction.

Apply the consequence if needed.
Move on.

That does not mean being robotic. It means staying calm, staying clear, and not giving the moment more energy than it deserves.

I also learned that follow-through works better when consequences are realistic.

Do not create consequences that depend on your anger. Use responses you can actually carry out. If I say, "If this happens again, I'm calling home," then I need to be ready to call home. If I say, "I will move seats," then I need to have another seat ready. If I say, "This will be documented," then I need to document it.

Follow-through works best when the teacher has already thought through what the next step is.

That is why it helps to decide ahead of time what your likely responses will be for common problems. For example:

- off-task talking may lead to a warning, then a seat change
- refusal to work may lead to a private conversation, documentation, and parent contact
- repeated interruptions may lead to redirection, consequence, and follow-up
- disrespect may require immediate correction, documentation, and a larger response depending on severity

The exact system may vary by teacher and school, but the principle stays the same: your response should not feel random.

Students should not feel like consequences appear out of nowhere. And teachers should not feel like they are improvising every boundary in the middle of stress.

I also believe follow-through should protect student dignity whenever possible.

Just because a consequence is necessary does not mean the moment needs to become public theater. In fact, many corrections land better when they are short, private, and direct. A student who wants attention from peers may only push harder if you correct them in front of everyone. But that same student may respond differently if you speak quietly, stay firm, and remove the audience from the moment.

That is why I believe in correcting with dignity.

Firm does not have to mean humiliating.

Students remember how adults respond to them. They remember whether correction felt respectful or performative. They remember whether the teacher seemed in control or just angry.

That is why follow-through and dignity need to work together.

One practical area where this mattered a lot for me was parent communication.

If I told a student I was going to contact home, I needed to do it.

Not three days later if I remembered.
Not only if I got more annoyed.

I needed to do it.

That helped students understand that my words had weight. It also helped families see that I was addressing concerns clearly instead of only reaching out when things had already gotten worse.

Always document behavior, including the date.

Documentation is part of follow-through. It keeps patterns from turning into vague impressions. It lets you say: this happened on these days, I responded this way, I contacted home, I changed the seat assignment, I gave the warning, and the pattern continued.

That record becomes important if you need support later.
It also keeps you grounded in facts instead of frustration.

Another lesson I had to learn was that follow-through is not about winning.

If a teacher starts seeing every correction as a battle to win, the room gets heavy fast. Students feel that energy. The teacher feels it too. Then every small issue starts feeling personal.

That is not sustainable.

Follow-through is not about proving that I am stronger than the student. It is about protecting the learning environment. It is about keeping expectations real. It is about helping the room stay teachable.

That mindset helped me.

Instead of thinking, I need to show them I am in charge, I started thinking, I need to keep the room safe, teachable, and clear.

That is a better frame.

It keeps the teacher in a leadership position instead of a reactive one.

And honestly, follow-through became easier for me once I stopped overexplaining everything. Students do not need a long lecture every time they cross a line. Most of the time, they already know what happened.

What they are learning now is whether I mean what I said.

That is the part that shapes the room.

This does not mean every consequence will work immediately. It will not. Some students will still test you. Some will resist. Some will complain. Some will act like they do not care.

But even then, follow-through still counts.

Because the goal is not to guarantee instant compliance every single time. The goal is to build a classroom where your words carry weight over time.

That is how your words start to carry weight.

What I eventually understood is this: every time I failed to follow through, I made the next correction harder. Every time I followed through calmly, I made the next correction clearer.

That is why follow-through matters so much.

Expectations matter.
Routines matter.
But without follow-through, both of them start to weaken.

Follow-through is what gives structure its backbone.

What I Learned

Students take expectations more seriously when they know my words have weight. Follow-through did not mean being harsh, but it did mean acting calmly and reliably when I said something would happen. The more I followed through, the stronger the room became.

Why This Works

Follow-through teaches students that expectations are real, not optional. When consequences are clear, calm, and carried out, students know the boundary is real. That reduces repeated testing, cuts down on negotiation, and makes the classroom easier to lead.

It also protects the teacher.

Less repeating.
Less negotiating.
Less emotional exhaustion.

Try This Tomorrow

Think about one behavior you keep correcting without fully following through on.

Ask yourself:

- What do I usually say in that moment?
- What is my actual next step if the behavior continues?
- Is that consequence realistic and ready to use?

Then choose one response you will follow through on calmly tomorrow.

Say less.

Mean it.

Act on it.

My Next Move

Where in my classroom am I giving more warnings than I am actually following through?

____

____

____

____

If You Want to Go Deeper: *Lee Canter's Assertive Discipline provides a helpful framework for follow-through that balances firmness with fairness. It is especially useful for teachers who struggle with consistency.*

Chapter 8
Be Consistent So Students Trust You

One of the most important things I have learned about classroom management is this: students pay attention to patterns.

They notice what you correct.
They notice what you ignore.
They notice what you say matters.
And they notice whether it still matters tomorrow.

That is why consistency matters so much.

Not because teachers have to be robotic.
Not because every moment should look exactly the same.
And not because good teaching means acting like a machine.

Consistency matters because students need to know that your words and actions match over time.

I think this is one of the biggest challenges for teachers, especially new teachers. Usually, it is not that they do not care. It is that they are trying to do too many things at once. They are teaching, watching behavior, managing time, answering questions, redirecting students, trying to stay calm, and trying not to forget what they already said five minutes earlier.

That is a lot.

So yes, consistency is harder than it sounds.

But it still matters.

Because when a teacher is inconsistent, students feel it quickly. If I correct talking one day and ignore it the next, students notice. If I let one student slide but come down hard on another for the same thing, students notice that too. And what they learn is not the expectation.

They learn that my words are optional.

That is the real damage of inconsistency.

As Marzano points out, students respond better when the teacher is reliable. Not perfect, but reliable. When students believe the room is fair and predictable, disruption tends to decrease and cooperation increases.

That is why credibility matters so much.

Once credibility starts to drop, classroom management gets harder than it needs to be. Students are no longer just responding to the expectation. They are testing whether the expectation is real.

That changes the room.

I think some teachers assume students mainly respect the loudest teacher or the strictest teacher. I do not think that is usually true.

A lot of the time, students respect the teacher they trust the most.

The teacher who means what they say.
The teacher who does not change the standard every day.

The teacher who does not threaten things they will not do.
The teacher who does not hand out random consequences depending on mood.
The teacher who feels grounded.

That kind of teacher earns trust.

And students respond differently to that.

Because credibility reduces confusion.

If students know what matters in the room, what happens when a line is crossed, and what the teacher is likely to do next, they spend less time guessing and less time testing. The room becomes easier to lead because the pattern starts doing some of the work.

That is what many teachers need.

Not more speeches.
Not more dramatic warnings.
Not more emotional effort.

A stronger pattern.

That is what consistency creates.

I also had to learn that consistency does not mean correcting everything with the exact same energy. That would not be realistic, and it would not be wise. Not every behavior deserves the same response.

A side conversation is not the same as open defiance.
A tired student having one off moment is not the same as a repeated pattern.
A small distraction is not the same as something unsafe.

Consistency is not sameness.

Consistency means the classroom still makes sense.

It means students can see a pattern in how you lead:

- expectations are taught
- boundaries are real
- redirection happens when needed
- consequences are not random
- fairness matters
- follow-through is normal

That fairness matters more than some teachers realize.

Students do not expect teachers to treat every person exactly the same, because students are not the same. But they do notice very quickly if the standard changes depending on who did it.

If one student gets a consequence because they are "always the problem," but another student does the same thing and gets a pass because that behavior is unusual for them, the room notices.

Students are always watching for that.

They are watching to see whether fairness is real, whether expectations apply to everyone, and whether the teacher is responding to behavior or to reputation.

That does not mean teacher judgment disappears.

Context still matters.
Patterns still matter.
Relationships still matter.

But the standard itself has to feel stable.

Students should not feel like they are being measured with different rulers depending on who they are, how much the teacher likes them, or what kind of mood the teacher is in that day.

That weakens credibility fast.

I also learned that consistency does not mean rigidity.

Sometimes good teaching requires flexibility. Sometimes a student asks for something, and the teacher has to decide whether saying yes, with clear conditions, might actually help.

That is still part of strong classroom management.

I had a student I will call Penelope. She talked constantly. It did not matter where I moved her—she would always find someone to talk to, and if she could not, she would probably start talking to the wall. Because she was so distracted, she often turned in work late, and when I asked questions, she often could not answer them.

Penelope had her best friend in class too. I will call her Lilly.

Lilly was the complete opposite. She was quiet, responsible, and focused.

Penelope asked me more than once if she could sit near Lilly. At first, I said no, because I assumed Penelope would just talk to her too and get even more distracted. Later she asked again, and I told her I would think about it. This was near the end of one marking period, and I usually like to change seats when a new marking period starts because it gives the room a reset.

After that, Penelope asked me every day if I had made a decision. Finally, I told her yes. I was going to let her sit near Lilly, but with a clear condition: if I had to redirect her even once for talking or being off task, I would move her immediately. I also told her I wanted to see improvement in turning in her work on time.

I knew Lilly was very responsible, so I thought she might help Penelope stay focused instead of pulling her further off task.

That is exactly what happened.

Penelope made a complete turnaround. I did not have to move her again. Her focus improved, her work improved, and both students handled their classroom jobs well.

It turned out to be a good decision. A few weeks before the end of the school year, I spoke with both students and told them I was proud of their progress and glad I had made that decision. They left my classroom feeling proud of themselves and happy.

Now, I am not saying this works every time. Sometimes flexibility backfires. Sometimes the original plan was right.

But I learned something important from that situation: sometimes a thoughtful adjustment, with clear limits, works better than an automatic no.

And if it does not work, you can always go back to the original plan.

That is not weakness.

That is judgment.

And judgment is part of consistency too.

I saw this play out again with a group of boys in one of my classes. They were constantly talking, disrupting instruction, distracting each other, and feeding off each other's energy. For weeks, I kept warning them, repeating myself, and getting frustrated.

Nothing changed.

Then one day, I pulled all four of them into the hallway.

I asked them directly, "Are you meeting the expectations of this classroom?"

They all admitted they were not.

I told them I was giving them one chance to improve.

Then I acted.

I changed every one of their seats. I gave one of them, a student with ADHD, anxiety, and behavioral challenges, a classroom role that kept him actively involved. I thanked him every day. I recognized his effort openly.

After that conversation and those changes, I never had to refer any of those boys.

By the end of the year, I emailed each of their parents to tell them how much their sons had improved.

Consistency was not just about correction.

It was about following through on the boundary and continuing to believe they could do better.

That is the kind of consistency students trust.

I think teachers sometimes lose consistency because they are reacting to the feeling of the day instead of the standard of the room.

That is understandable.

Some days you are tired.
Some classes are harder.

Some periods push more than others.
Some moments catch you when your patience is already low.

But students should not have to guess which version of the teacher they are getting.

If the standard changes every time the teacher's mood changes, the room becomes unstable.

And unstable rooms create more testing, not less.

Because students keep checking:

- Does this still matter today?
- Does it matter in this class period?
- Does it matter with this student?
- Does it matter when the teacher is tired?
- Does it matter when the teacher is busy?

If the answer keeps changing, credibility weakens.

That is why consistency protects authority.

It keeps authority from depending only on personality, emotion, or energy.

I also think consistency helps consequences land better. When consequences seem random, students experience them as personal. When consequences are tied to clear patterns, they make more sense. Students may still dislike them, but they understand them better.

That matters.

Because one of the fastest ways to lose a classroom is to make students feel like your reactions are unpredictable.

Unpredictable teachers create anxious rooms.
Predictable teachers create calmer rooms.

And calmer rooms are easier to lead.

I also learned that inconsistency creates extra work.

When expectations are not enforced consistently, the teacher has to keep re-explaining, re-warning, re-negotiating, and re-proving the same thing. The room becomes more tiring because every boundary has to be rebuilt over and over again.

That drains a teacher fast.

Consistency saves energy.

Not because it makes the job easy.
But because it reduces how often you have to restart the same battle.

If students already know:

- phone use means this
- side conversations mean this
- unfinished work means this
- disrespect means this
- transitions should look like this

then the teacher does not have to reinvent authority every day.

That is a much better way to live.

I also think consistency helps teachers feel stronger.

Not just look stronger.
Feel stronger.

Because when you know your expectations, know your response patterns, and know the room is not being run by mood, you do not have to rely as much on emotion in the moment. You do not have to invent your authority. You do not have to prove it every five minutes.

You just lead the room.

That is more sustainable.

It saves energy.
It protects your credibility.
It reduces power struggles.
It helps students feel more secure.
It makes your classroom feel more dependable.

If I had to say it simply, I would say this:

Students do not need constant intensity.

They need patterns they can trust.

That is what consistency gives them.

And over time, those patterns build something very important: credibility.

Once students believe that your expectations are real, your responses are fair, and your leadership is dependable, the classroom becomes easier to lead.

Not because students stop being kids.

But because they know who you are.
They know what matters.
They know what your words mean.
And they know the room is not being run by unpredictability.

What I Learned

Students trust a teacher whose words and actions match. Consistency did not mean handling every situation exactly the same way, but it did mean staying fair, steady, and believable. The more predictable I became, the more stable the classroom became.

Why This Works

Students respond better when the classroom feels reliable. Consistency lowers confusion, strengthens credibility, and helps students understand that expectations are real. It also makes consequences feel less personal because students can see the pattern behind them.

Consistency does not remove judgment. It gives judgment a steady framework.

Try This Tomorrow

Think about one expectation in your classroom that may feel unclear because your response has not been consistent.

Then choose one area to tighten tomorrow. Keep the response clear, calm, and repeatable.

Do not try to fix everything at once. Strengthen one pattern first.

My Next Move

Where in my classroom do students need more steadiness from me so they can trust my leadership?

____

____

____

____

If You Want to Go Deeper: *Robert J. Marzano, Jana S. Marzano, and Debra J. Pickering's Classroom Management That Works offers one of the clearest research-based explanations of why consistency, fairness, and predictability matter so much in the classroom. It is especially helpful for teachers who want to understand not just what works, but why it works.*

Chapter 9
Use a Quiet System to Stay Consistent

One of the biggest classroom management mistakes I made early on was talking too much when I needed students' attention.

I would try to start talking while students were still settling.
Then I would repeat myself.
Then I would wait and try again.
Then I would start giving reminders.
And by the time I actually began, I was already frustrated.

That cycle was exhausting.

It also was not helping. The more I talked just to get the room quiet, the less effective my voice became. And when students were never quite sure how I was going to get their attention, transitions into instruction felt slower, messier, and less consistent.

That is one reason I needed a system.

Not a dramatic one.
Not a punishment-heavy one.
A clear one.

I needed something that would help me stay consistent without turning every small behavior issue into a whole-class interruption. I needed something students could understand quickly and something I could actually follow through on.

That is when I started using sticky notes as part of my warning system.

It is simple, but it has helped me a lot.

When a student is talking, off task, or being disruptive, I can give a verbal warning or quietly place a sticky note with the number 1 on the student's desk.

That is the first warning.

If the behavior continues, I place a second sticky note with the number 2 on the desk.

That is the second warning.

There is no third sticky note.

If I have already given two warnings and the behavior continues, the student stays with me at the end of class for a reflection or conversation. If the same behavior continues across future classes, I move to parent contact. If it continues after that, it becomes a referral.

That is the system.

Warning.
Reflection or conversation.
Parent contact.
Referral.

What helped me most is that the system is quiet.

It does not require me to stop the lesson and give a speech.
It does not require me to embarrass the student in front of everyone else.
It does not require me to keep repeating myself while the whole room watches.

It lets me respond clearly and keep teaching.

Students at this age are highly sensitive to public correction. Some shut down when they feel embarrassed. Some become defensive. Some start performing for peers. Some escalate because now the whole room is watching.

That is one reason I prefer low-drama systems whenever possible.

I do not want every correction to become a scene.

A sticky note does not solve everything, but it helps me address behavior without making the moment bigger than it needs to be.

It also helps me stay calmer.

If I already know what step comes next, I do not have to improvise in frustration. I do not have to decide in the moment whether I am serious this time. I do not have to search for the right words while my patience gets thinner.

The system carries part of that weight for me.

Students also respond better when they understand the system ahead of time.

I do not just start placing sticky notes on desks without explanation. I teach the system when I teach expectations. I explain what the warnings mean. I explain what happens after the second warning. I explain that there is no third sticky note. I explain what reflection time looks like. I explain when parent contact or a referral may happen.

They may not like the system.
They may still test it.
But they should understand it.

That clarity helps the classroom feel more fair.

One of the clearest examples of this happened during my first year of teaching. I had a student who always wanted to be the center of attention. He made constant noises, found ways to distract other students, and looked for reactions all day long. Sometimes he used objects. Sometimes he used his mouth. Even his shoes became part of the disruption.

At the time, I gave him too much attention for the wrong behavior. I corrected him over and over, reacted in the moment, and without meaning to, I fed the pattern. The more attention the behavior got, the more chaos it created.

What finally helped was putting my system into place.

When he was talking, off task, or trying to entertain the class, I could give a verbal warning or quietly place a sticky note with the number 1 on his desk. If the behavior continued, I placed a second sticky note, marked with a 2, on his desk.

That let me respond without stopping instruction, arguing across the room, or turning the moment into a performance.

I also started using more proximity.

Sometimes I would walk near him while I kept teaching. Sometimes I would pause by his desk for a second. Sometimes that alone was enough to stop the behavior before it grew.

That combination helped.

The sticky notes gave the correction structure.
Proximity gave it quiet support.
Using the system consistently made it work.

That is what I needed.

Because for me, the issue was not only knowing that a student was off task. Usually I knew that. The harder part was knowing how to respond without overtalking, overreacting, or feeding the behavior with too much public attention.

This system helped me do that.

It also helped me stop living in endless verbal warnings.

That matters because too much talking weakens correction. If students hear the same warning again and again without anything changing, they start tuning it out. The teacher ends up talking more and meaning less.

A quiet system interrupts that.

It gives the warning a shape.
It gives the consequence a path.
It gives the teacher something to rely on besides frustration.

I also like that this system leaves room for dignity.

A student does not have to be publicly called out every time they are off task. A quiet correction often works better. It protects the student from unnecessary embarrassment, and it protects the class from getting pulled into someone else's moment.

That matters more than some teachers realize.

Not every student who is off task needs a public confrontation.
Not every redirection needs a speech.
Not every correction needs an audience.

Sometimes a sticky note says enough.

Another reason this system works for me is that it creates a pause before bigger consequences.

Instead of jumping from irritation to a major response, I can move through a clear progression. The student sees that there was a warning. Then another warning. Then the next step.

That helps consequences feel less random.

It also helps me stay grounded in what actually happened instead of what I felt in the moment.

That is important.

A good system should protect the teacher from impulsive reactions just as much as it protects students from unpredictable ones.

I also think the conversation or reflection after class can make a real difference.

That step gives the student a chance to think, reset, and hear the message more clearly without the audience of peers. It also reminds the student that the warning was not empty.

Sometimes that conversation is short.

You were warned twice.
The behavior continued.
What needs to change next class?

Sometimes I ask the student to reflect briefly in writing. Sometimes I keep it verbal. The format is less important than the clarity behind it.

The goal is not to drag the moment out.

The goal is to make the next step real.

That is important because many students are used to warnings that go nowhere. A quiet system helps break that pattern.

It also helps the student see that the consequence is connected to behavior, not just to teacher frustration.

I do not believe every consequence has to be huge to be effective. In fact, many classroom consequences work better when they are small, immediate, and consistent.

That is one reason I like this system.

It is not dramatic.
It is not extreme.
But it gives the teacher a clear ladder to follow.

And that progression matters.

Because one of the hardest parts of classroom management is not knowing what to do next.

Teachers often get stuck in one of two places:

Either they overreact too fast,
or they keep giving endless warnings and do nothing.

Neither one works well.

A clear system helps the teacher avoid both extremes. It gives students a chance to correct the behavior without turning consequences into empty threats. And it gives the classroom more structure.

I also want to say this clearly: a system only works if you actually use it.

If I give a sticky note and then ignore the continued behavior, the note means nothing.
If I say the student will stay after class and then let it go, the whole ladder weakens.
If I say I will contact home and then never do it, students notice that too.

So yes, the sticky notes help.

But what really makes the system work is consistency.

Students learn quickly whether a system is real. They learn whether the steps actually lead somewhere. And if they do, the classroom gets stronger over time.

Another reason I like this system is that it gives me options.

Not every student needs the exact same response every day. Sometimes I give the warning verbally. Sometimes I use the sticky note. Sometimes the brief reflection after class is enough. Sometimes I already know the pattern is repeated enough that I need to contact home.

The goal is not to become mechanical.

The goal is to stop being random.

That distinction is important.

A system should support teacher judgment, not replace it. But it should protect the teacher from having to reinvent consequences every time a student gets off track.

That is what this system has done for me.

It has helped me stay quieter.
Clearer.
More consistent.
Less reactive.
And more able to correct behavior without turning every moment into a power struggle.

That is why I believe in low-drama systems.

They support the teacher.
They preserve the student's dignity.
And they protect instructional time.

If I could say it simply, I would say this:

Students do not need a teacher who keeps repeating the same warning louder and louder.

They need a teacher whose system makes the next step clear.

That is what the sticky notes gave me.

Not perfection.

Just a clearer path.

What I Learned

I became more consistent when I stopped relying on repeated verbal warnings and started using a clear, quiet system. The sticky notes did not solve every behavior problem, but they helped me correct students with less emotion, less repetition, and more follow-through.

Why This Works

A quiet system lowers drama and increases clarity. Students know what each step means, and the teacher does not have to keep improvising in the moment. That makes correction feel more predictable, more private, and less emotional.

It also protects instruction.
The lesson keeps moving.
The teacher stays calmer.
The response stays clear.

Try This Tomorrow

Think about one behavior you correct too often with too many words.

Ask yourself:

- What is my current warning system?
- Do students clearly understand the steps?
- What quiet signal or response could replace repeated talking?
- What happens after the warning?

Then build one simple response you can use consistently. Keep it clear, visible, and easy to follow through on.

Less talking.
More clarity.
More consistency.

My Next Move

What classroom behavior would improve if I replaced repeated verbal warnings with a clear, quiet system?

____

____

____

____

If You Want to Go Deeper: *Doug Lemov's Teach Like a Champion offers dozens of specific techniques for tightening routines, transitions, and classroom systems. It is one of the most actionable classroom management books available.*

Chapter 10
Stay in Control Without Raising Your Voice

One of the biggest misconceptions about classroom management is that authority has to sound loud.

I understand why many teachers fall into that idea, especially at the beginning. When students are talking over you, ignoring directions, feeding off each other's energy, or pushing a lesson off track, it can feel like the only way to regain the room is to get louder than they are.

That instinct makes sense.

But it does not lead to the kind of authority most teachers actually want.

I learned early on that louder does not automatically mean stronger. In fact, for many teachers, it means the opposite. It can be a sign that the moment is starting to pull them out of position instead of reinforcing their leadership.

That was an important shift for me.

Earlier in my career, there were days when I tried to compete with the noise in the room by talking louder and louder, and by the end of the day I had almost no voice left. I thought volume would make me sound more authoritative. I assumed that if students felt more force in my voice, they would take me more seriously.

But volume did not create the kind of authority I was actually looking for. It raised the emotional temperature of the room, strained my voice, and still did not solve the deeper problem.

I still remember one day early in my career when I raised my voice at a class that would not stop talking. The room went quiet, but not in the way I wanted. Students froze. A few looked uncomfortable. One girl near the front put her head down.

I had gotten silence, but I had not really gotten control.

After class, one student stayed behind and said quietly, "Miss, you scared me."

She was not being dramatic.

She meant it.

That moment stayed with me. I realized that silence born from fear is not the same as a classroom that is functioning. From that point on, I started working on becoming the calmest voice in the room, not the loudest.

Because volume is not the same as control.
And frustration is not the same as authority.

A teacher can be loud and still have a weak classroom system.
A teacher can be calm and still have a very strong room.

That difference changed the way I teach.

Fred Jones makes this point well: many of the strongest classroom managers rely less on repeated verbal correction and more on movement, proximity, body language, and calm presence. Very often, the teachers with the quietest rooms are not the loudest teachers. They are the clearest and calmest ones.

I am not saying teachers will never raise their voice. Sometimes a situation is unsafe. Sometimes something needs to stop immediately. Sometimes a sharper tone is necessary in the moment.

That is different.

What I mean is this: yelling should not be your classroom management system.

Students should not only know you are serious when you get loud. They should know you are serious because your expectations are clear, your directions are direct, your tone is firm, and your follow-through is real.

That kind of authority lasts longer.

I think this matters especially in Grades 6–9 because students at this age are highly responsive to emotional energy. If the teacher starts escalating, the room often escalates too. Some students shut down. Some get defensive. Some get embarrassed. Some get louder. Some start watching the conflict instead of paying attention to the lesson.

Now the room is no longer just off track.

Now it is emotionally charged.

And emotionally charged classrooms are much harder to lead well.

That is why I believe calm matters so much.

A calm teacher is not a weak teacher.

That needs to be said clearly, because many people still confuse calm with passive. They think that if a teacher is not yelling, then the teacher is too soft. They think seriousness has to sound intense. They think authority has to feel dramatic.

I do not agree with that.

A calm teacher can still be firm.
A calm teacher can still stop a room.
A calm teacher can still correct behavior immediately.
A calm teacher can still hold a very clear boundary.

In fact, I think staying calm often takes more control than yelling.

Students notice when the adult in the room is emotionally grounded. They may not describe it that way, but they feel it. They notice when the teacher does not panic. They notice when the teacher does not get dragged into chaos. They notice when the teacher's words still carry weight without needing a performance of anger.

That matters because long-term authority is not built on intensity.

It is built on consistency.

Students learn a pattern:

- the teacher notices
- the teacher responds
- the teacher means what they say
- the teacher follows through
- the teacher does not get pulled into every emotional trap

That kind of pattern builds trust in the room.

Students may not always like it, but they learn it.

I also had to learn that if I ever felt myself wanting to get louder, I needed to ask a harder question:

What is actually managing the room right now, my system or my frustration?

That question matters.

Because if a classroom only works when the teacher keeps getting louder, then it is not really being held together by strong management.

It is being held together by escalation.

And escalation wears everyone down.

It wears down the teacher, and it wears down the students.

I do not want my stress to become the structure.

I want the structure to be the structure.

That is why strong classroom management starts before the moment when a teacher feels tempted to yell.

It starts with:

- clear expectations
- practiced routines
- strong transitions
- consistent follow-through
- brief correction
- early redirection

- consequences that do not depend on emotion

Those things reduce the need to raise your voice.

Not perfectly.
Not every time.
But often enough to make a difference.

I also think yelling can blur the message.

Students may hear the emotion but miss the direction. They may focus on the teacher's frustration instead of their own behavior. They may feel embarrassed instead of corrected. They may react to the tone more than the actual issue.

That rarely helps.

Especially with adolescents.

Students at this age are often reactive. They are also watching to see whether the adult in the room can stay calm under pressure. Many are sensitive to embarrassment and quick to perform for peers. If the teacher turns every difficult moment into a loud public scene, students often remember the scene more than the lesson behind it.

That is not effective classroom management.

A room can get quiet because the teacher exploded.

But silence after an explosion is not the same as a healthy classroom.

Sometimes students get quiet because they froze.
Sometimes they get quiet because the room got uncomfortable.
Sometimes they get quiet because the moment turned tense.

That is not the kind of authority I would want to build a classroom on.

I would rather build a classroom where students know calm still means serious.

That takes consistency.

Students need to learn that when I speak calmly, I still mean what I say. A calm redirection is still a real redirection. A calm consequence is still a real consequence. A calm boundary is still a boundary.

That is where many teachers get stuck.

Because calm by itself is not enough.

Calm without follow-through becomes weak.
But calm with consistency is strong.

That is an important difference.

I also think body language matters more than many teachers realize.

Some teachers assume volume is the main way to communicate authority, but students read much more than volume. They notice whether you pause, whether you wait, whether you move with purpose, whether your posture changes, whether your face changes, whether you look steady or frantic, and whether you act like you expect to be heard.

That matters.

A teacher who pauses, stands still, looks at the class, and gives a clear direction can often communicate more authority than a teacher who is loudly talking over students.

Yelling over noise keeps you inside the noise.

Calm control helps you rise above it.

I also want to say something clearly for new teachers: if you feel like you have to get louder to prove you are in charge, I understand the temptation. I really do.

When you are trying to hold the room, especially in the beginning, loudness can feel like the fastest tool available.

But fast is not always effective.

What helped me more was not getting louder.

It was getting clearer.

Clearer expectations.
Clearer directions.
Clearer consequences.
Clearer follow-through.

That changed much more than volume ever did.

I think one of the most important shifts in classroom management is when a teacher realizes this:

I do not need to be louder. I need to be clearer.

That changes a lot.

Because clarity leads to consistency.
Consistency builds credibility.
And credibility creates authority.

That authority is more stable than volume.

And honestly, it feels better too.

It feels better to leave class knowing you stayed in control of yourself. It feels better to know your students responded because your systems were stronger, not because your frustration got louder than theirs.

And it feels better to lead the room without feeling like you had to fight for it with your voice.

That does not mean every day will be easy.

There will still be difficult classes.
There will still be frustrating moments.
There will still be times when students test you.

The goal is not to become emotionless.

The goal is to become more intentional.
To pause sooner.
To correct earlier.
To rely on structure more than emotion.
To use your tone with purpose.
To make your calm stronger than their chaos.

That is real leadership in the classroom.

And I think students need it.

Many students already live around enough yelling, enough unpredictability, and enough emotional intensity. They do not need more of that in the classroom. They need structure. They need clarity. They need steadiness. They need an adult who can lead the room without losing themselves in the process.

For me, learning not to rely on volume was part of learning how to lead with more self-control. It taught me to trust structure more than emotion, clarity more than loudness, and consistency more than intensity.

And in the long run, I think it made me stronger.

Not because I became louder.
But because I stopped believing loud was the same thing as control.

What I Learned

I used to think volume would help me sound more authoritative, but it did not give me the kind of control I actually wanted. Real authority came from calm, clarity, and follow-through. The stronger my systems became, the less I needed my voice to carry the weight of the room.

Why This Works

When a teacher stays calm, students are more likely to hear the correction instead of reacting to the teacher's emotion. A calm voice keeps the situation from getting bigger. It also shows students that the teacher is in control of the room and of themselves.

Calm works best when it is paired with action.

If the teacher gives a direction, waits, and follows through, students learn that yelling is not necessary for the message to be serious.

Try This Tomorrow

Pick one moment when students usually get loud, get off task, or become hard to redirect.

When it happens:

- stop talking
- stand still
- make eye contact with the students who need the correction

- give one short direction
- do not repeat yourself more than once
- if they still do not respond, follow through with the next step

You can say:

> "Stop talking."
>
> "Go back to your seat."
>
> "This is your warning."
>
> "Now you need to move."

Keep your voice calm. Keep your words short. Let the follow-through do the work.

My Next Move

What classroom moment most often pulls me toward raising my voice instead of staying clear and calm?

____

____

____

____

If You Want to Go Deeper: *Fred Jones's Tools for Teaching is especially helpful for understanding how calm presence, body language, proximity, and clear systems can manage behavior more effectively than volume. It is a strong resource for teachers who want to lead with more authority without relying on yelling, repeated verbal correction, or emotional escalation.*

Chapter 11
Notice the Students Who Are Doing the Right Thing

One of the easiest mistakes to make in classroom management is giving most of our attention to the students who struggle the most to manage themselves.

I understand why that happens. Disruptive behavior gets our attention fast. It interrupts instruction. It creates stress. It demands an immediate response. By the end of the day, it can feel like all of our energy went to the students who needed the most redirection.

But there is another group of students in the room, and they matter too.

They are the students who come in ready to learn. They settle in quickly. They follow directions. They are responsible. They are kind. They try. They are not perfect, but they show up willing to do what is expected.

Those students are easy to overlook.

Not because we do not care about them, but because they are not pulling the room off track. They are quietly doing what they are supposed to do while someone else takes most of our attention.

Over time, that can send the wrong message.

If the only students who get repeated attention are the ones who are off task, defiant, loud, or disruptive, the students who are doing the right thing can start to feel invisible. They notice who gets the teacher's time. They notice who gets the conversation. They notice who gets the follow-up.

And they notice when their consistency goes unseen.

I learned this in a very personal way during my first year of teaching.

One of my most difficult classes was my seventh-period group. They were extremely loud, full of energy, and very hard to settle. Most of the class was made up of boys, many of them athletes, and at that point I did not yet have the structure or experience to lead that room well. Too often, the noise and disorder set the tone instead of me.

What stayed with me most, though, was not only how hard that class felt for me.

It was what that kind of environment meant for the students who were ready to learn.

At the end of the year, I received several kind notes from students. One of them came from a girl I will call Bekka. She was quiet, respectful, and always ready to learn. In her note, Bekka wrote, "Mrs. Granado, I hope your next school year is much better and that you get better students. You are a great teacher, and I learned a lot from you."

Her note encouraged me, but it also made me reflect. I had spent so much of that year trying to manage the room that I often felt I had not taught students like Bekka as well as I should have. She came ready to learn, and I know she was not the only one. But because I did not yet know how to create enough structure in that class, the disorder often took over. Students like her were there, but they did not get the classroom they deserved.

That stayed with me. It made me realize that classroom management is not only about correcting the students who are struggling. It is also about protecting the learning environment for the students who are trying.

That is part of the work too.

I told myself then, This cannot keep happening.

And I have worked hard to make sure it does not.

That is why I believe in being intentional about noticing what is going right.

I do not mean that every good choice needs a prize. I do not mean students need constant public praise. In Grades 6–9, that can backfire. Students at this age still need affirmation, but they often do not want attention in front of everyone else. Public praise can embarrass them, even when they appreciate it.

That is why I usually keep it direct and personal.

A quiet comment can go a long way.

"I noticed how focused you were today."
"Thank you for getting started right away."
"I can count on you."
"You handled that really well."

Those small comments matter more than we sometimes realize. Students at this age may act like they do not care, but they do. They want to be seen. They want to know their effort matters. They want to know someone noticed.

I also like to send positive emails home.

If I need to send an email to a parent about behavior, I also try to send one or two positive emails home. That helps me keep perspective. It reminds me that even on hard days, not everything is going wrong.

Sometimes the email is very simple:

"I'm very happy to have your child in my class. They consistently come to class ready to learn, and they are responsible and kind. Your support at home is evident, and I truly appreciate your partnership."

Those small messages go a long way.

They encourage students.
They strengthen trust with families.
And they remind me to notice the good in the room.

There are still students showing responsibility, effort, growth, and kindness.

There is still good in the room.

And that reminder helps me too.

It keeps me from becoming so focused on correction that I forget gratitude. It reminds me to appreciate what is going well instead of only reacting to what is not. Classroom management is not only about addressing problems. It is also about reinforcing the behaviors and habits we want to see more of.

That matters because what gets noticed gets repeated.

When students learn that responsibility, effort, and self-control are seen, those things gain value in the room. Not in a fake or performative way. In a real way.

Students understand what matters by watching where the teacher's attention goes.

If my attention only goes to disruption, then disruption starts to feel central.
If my attention also goes to responsibility, then responsibility becomes more visible too.

That changes the tone of the classroom.

It also helps protect the students who are doing what they are supposed to do.

I think teachers sometimes forget how discouraging it can feel for a responsible student to sit in a room where the same few students keep getting most of the energy, most of the correction, and most of the attention. Even if that attention is negative, it still pulls the center of the room toward disruption.

That is not fair.

The students who are ready to learn deserve a classroom that sees them too.

They deserve a teacher who notices their consistency.
They deserve a classroom where effort is not invisible.
They deserve a learning environment that does not revolve only around the hardest behavior in the room.

That is one reason this chapter feels so important to me.

Noticing what is going right does not mean ignoring what is wrong.

It means not letting what is wrong become the only thing you see.

That distinction is important.

Because teachers can get emotionally trained to scan the room only for problems. We start looking for who is off task, who is talking, who is avoiding work, who is pushing limits, who needs redirection next. Some of that is necessary. But if that becomes our only lens, we miss a lot.

We miss the student who got started without being reminded.
We miss the student who stayed focused during a hard lesson.
We miss the student who showed kindness to someone else.
We miss the student who is not flashy but is steady every single day.

Those students matter.

And they should not have to become difficult before they become visible.

I also think this shapes the teacher's mindset.

When a class is hard, it is easy to leave the room thinking nothing went well. But often that is not fully true. Often there were still students trying. Still students showing respect. Still students doing their part. Noticing that helps me stay grounded.

It reminds me that the whole room is not chaos.
It reminds me that good is still happening.
It reminds me that the class is not defined only by its hardest moments.

That perspective is especially important on the days when correction feels heavy.

Students who are doing the right thing should not become invisible just because they are easier to teach.

They need encouragement too.

They need to know their choices matter.

And sometimes, we as teachers need that reminder too.

In every class, there is something good worth noticing.

What I Learned

I learned that if I was not careful, the most disruptive students could take up too much of my attention. That was understandable, but it was not healthy for the room. I had to be intentional about noticing the students who showed responsibility, kindness, and effort every day. They needed encouragement too. And honestly, so did I.

Why This Works

Students are more likely to repeat behaviors that are noticed and affirmed. Quiet, sincere recognition helps responsible students feel seen without embarrassing them. Positive communication with families also builds trust and helps create a classroom culture where good choices are visible and valued.

It also helps the teacher keep perspective.

Not everything is going wrong.
Not everyone is off task.
There is still a lot of good in the room.

Try This Tomorrow

Choose two students who are consistently making good choices and give each of them a short, sincere comment before the day is over.

Then take one more step:

- send one positive email home this week
- thank one student privately for being dependable
- notice one student who usually does the right thing quietly
- look for effort, not just perfection

Do this especially on a day when you also have to address difficult behavior. That is often when you need the reminder most.

My Next Move

Who in my classroom is consistently doing the right thing, and have I let that go unnoticed?

____

____

____

____

If You Want to Go Deeper: *For one week, pay attention to which students get most of your correction, most of your conversation, and most of your emotional energy. Then ask yourself whether your responsible students are being seen often enough. Classroom management is stronger when correction and encouragement work together.*

Chapter 12
Don't Take Behavior Personally

One of the hardest things I had to learn as a teacher was not to take student behavior personally.

That sounds simple.

It is not.

When a student rolls their eyes, talks back, ignores directions, gives attitude, or acts like they do not care, it is easy to feel disrespected. It is easy to take that moment straight to the heart. It can feel like the student is challenging you, rejecting you, or trying to make your job harder on purpose.

And sometimes students do make rude choices.

Sometimes they are disrespectful.
Sometimes they are testing limits.
Sometimes they are frustrated and handle it badly.

But even then, I had to learn something important:

Not everything is about me.

A student's behavior may need correction, but that does not mean it is a personal attack I need to carry with me all day.

That shift changed a lot for me.

As Tom Bennett writes in *Running the Room*, strong teachers learn to maintain what he calls emotional sobriety—not detachment, but the ability to respond without being destabilized by student behavior. That idea stayed with me. It does not mean you feel nothing. It means you do not let what you feel run the room.

At the beginning, I think I was too emotionally tied to student behavior. If a student was rude, I felt hurt. If a student pushed back, I felt challenged. If a student acted annoyed with me, I felt like I had done something wrong or like I had to prove I was in control.

That mindset made classroom management harder.

Because when you take everything personally, you are more likely to react emotionally. You get offended faster. You get louder faster. You stay in the moment longer than you need to. And sometimes you turn one bad choice into a bigger conflict because now it is no longer just about the behavior.

Now it feels personal.

That is where a lot of power struggles begin.

What helped me was learning not to take student behavior as a measure of my worth as a teacher.

A student can be frustrated without that making me a bad teacher.
A student can be upset about correction without that meaning they hate me.
A student can have an attitude without my needing to absorb it and carry it into the rest of my day.

That does not make the behavior okay.
It just helps me respond more wisely.

And that matters.

I still believe in correction. I still believe in consequences. I still believe in follow-through. But I learned that I can correct a student without making the moment bigger than it needs to be.

I can address the behavior.
I can be clear.
I can hold the boundary.
I can give the consequence if needed.
Then I can move on.

That is a healthier way to teach.

This is especially important in classroom management because students at this age do not always act from maturity. They act from impulse, insecurity, embarrassment, peer pressure, frustration, attention-seeking, and poor judgment.

At this age, students are still learning how to regulate emotions, manage impulses, and respond well under pressure. That does not excuse disrespect or poor choices. But it does help explain why behavior is not always thoughtful, measured, or personal. Much of what teachers see in the classroom is immaturity colliding with emotion, peer dynamics, and underdeveloped self-control.

That does not excuse bad behavior.

But it does explain why teachers have to stay calm.

If I interpret every immature behavior as a personal statement about me, I will respond too emotionally. I will correct from wounded pride instead of clarity.

That hurts the classroom.

I had to learn that there is a difference between recognizing disrespect and internalizing every difficult moment.

A teacher can say, "That behavior is not acceptable," without turning it into something more personal: "This student is attacking me, and now I need to respond from that place."

Those are not the same thing.

One is professional clarity.
The other is emotional entanglement.

And classroom management becomes much harder when teachers become emotionally entangled in every difficult moment.

I think many teachers struggle with this because we care.

We care about our classrooms.
We care about doing well.
We care about being respected.
We care about our students.

So when students are rude, dismissive, or difficult, it lands.

Of course it does.

We are human.

But part of maturing in this work is learning not to let every student reaction define the moment for you.

Some behaviors are not really about you.

Sometimes a student is embarrassed.
Sometimes a student is trying to impress peers.
Sometimes a student is carrying anger from somewhere else.
Sometimes a student is frustrated with school, not with you

specifically.
Sometimes a student is simply immature.

Again, that does not make the behavior okay.

But it should change how we carry it.

Because if I know a student's behavior may be coming from a place bigger than me, I have a better chance of responding with calm instead of personal offense.

That is stronger.

I also think taking things personally pushes teachers toward the wrong goal.

Instead of asking, *What does this situation need?* we start asking, *How do I show this student they cannot do that to me?*

That is a dangerous shift.

Because now the moment is no longer centered on the classroom, the expectation, or the best response. Now it is centered on the teacher's pride.

And pride is not a good classroom management system.

It makes people react bigger than necessary.
It makes them talk too much.
It turns corrections into battles.

That usually does not help, especially in front of an audience.

Sometimes the student who wants to perform for the room will test you even more during an observation. The moment an administrator walks in, that student may push limits just to see what happens. That is exactly when your routines and expectations matter most. I do not ignore it, and I do not overreact. I stay calm, restate the expectation, and follow through if needed.

That helps me stay grounded.
And it helps the room keep moving.

I think this comes back to remembering who you are in the classroom.

You are the adult.

That means you cannot afford to react from the same emotional level as a student. If a student is annoyed, impulsive, embarrassed, dramatic, or disrespectful, you still have to stay calm enough to lead.

That is not always easy.

But it is necessary.

Because the moment you start reacting like another offended person in the room, you stop leading with clarity. You start defending yourself instead of managing the situation.

And students can tell.

They can tell when a teacher gets hooked.
They can tell when they can pull an emotional reaction.

I do not want one student's mood, attitude, or immaturity to decide mine.

That does not mean I feel nothing.

It means I try not to let the feeling drive the response.

That is a big difference.

I also think teachers need permission to admit that some student behavior does sting.

Not because we are weak.
Because we are human.

Some comments stay with you. Some moments feel insulting. Some days, student energy wears on you more than usual.

That is real.

But maturity is not pretending you are unaffected by everything.

It is learning how to feel something without letting it run the room.

That is real strength.

I also learned that when I take behavior personally, I start focusing too much on proving a point. I want the student to understand right now. I want the student to admit they were wrong. I want closure in the moment.

And that usually makes me talk too much.

Sometimes the strongest response is shorter.

"That is not acceptable."
"We are not doing this right now."
"You can speak to me after class."
"You can talk to me, but not like that."
"I have already given the direction."
"We will handle this later."

That kind of response protects your authority because it stays focused. It does not beg. It does not argue. It does not unravel emotionally in front of the class.

It leads.

One of the best questions a teacher can ask in a hard moment is this:

Am I responding to what happened, or to how personally I took it?

That is an uncomfortable question.

But it is a useful one.

Because sometimes what makes us react so strongly is not only the behavior itself. It is the story we attach to it.

They are trying to disrespect me.
They think I am weak.
They are making me look bad.

Sometimes that story is partly true.

But even then, you still have to decide whether reacting from that place will help you lead well.

Most of the time, it will not.

I also think teachers need emotional boundaries, not just classroom boundaries.

A classroom boundary says, *This behavior is not allowed here.*
An emotional boundary says, *I am not going to carry every student's behavior inside me like it defines my worth, my skill, or my whole day.*

Both are important.

Without classroom boundaries, the room gets messy.
Without emotional boundaries, the teacher gets drained.

And drained teachers make weaker decisions.

That is why this is so important.

If every rude comment lingers all day, if every eye roll feels like a deep insult, if every difficult class period makes you question yourself completely, this work will wear you down very quickly.

You cannot teach well when everything is getting under your skin all the time.

I also want to say this clearly: not taking things personally does not mean becoming cold or detached.

It does not mean lowering standards.
It does not mean tolerating disrespect.
It does not mean acting like nothing matters.

It means keeping enough emotional distance to stay wise.

That is the goal.

I can care without absorbing everything.
I can correct without taking the bait.
I can address disrespect without making it about my ego.
I can protect the room without carrying every moment like a wound.

That is healthier.

And honestly, it makes classroom management more effective too.

Because when teachers stop taking every behavior personally, they usually become more precise. They correct what needs correcting. They stop overexplaining. They stop escalating small moments. They stay calmer. They follow through better.

That makes the classroom steadier and easier to lead.

I also think not taking things personally helps teachers reset more quickly.

If a class period goes badly and I take it completely personally, then I carry that energy into the next class. My tone changes. My patience drops. My confidence dips. Now one hard group starts affecting everyone else.

Sometimes you have to mentally reset.

That class was difficult.
That student was rude.
That moment was frustrating.
But I am not going to let it carry into the rest of my day.

That kind of reset matters.

It protects your energy.
It protects your next group of students.
It protects your perspective.

If I could say it simply, I would say this: not everything students do is about you, and even when something feels personal, carrying it personally will rarely help you lead well.

A better set of questions is this:

- What is the right response?
- What does the room need?
- What boundary needs to be clear?
- What do I need to let go of so I can keep teaching well?

Those are stronger questions.

They keep you in the adult role.
They keep your ego from leading.

They protect your energy.
They protect the classroom.

And over time, that makes you stronger.

Not because students stop being difficult.
But because you stop letting every difficult moment define you.

What I Learned

I learned that taking student behavior personally made me more reactive and less effective. The more I separated student behavior from my own identity, the more clearly I could correct, follow through, and move on. That made me steadier, and it made the classroom easier to lead.

Why This Works

When teachers stop taking behavior personally, they respond with more clarity, clearer boundaries, and better judgment. That helps them avoid power struggles, protect their energy, and handle difficult moments more wisely.

Try This Tomorrow

The next time a student gives attitude or talks back, pause before responding. Keep your words short, address the behavior, give the direction, and move on.

You can say:

- "You can talk to me, but not like that."
- "You can speak to me after class."
- "I have already given the direction."

Do not try to win the moment.

Try to lead it.

My Next Move

What student behavior am I most likely to take personally, and how can I respond more professionally the next time?

____

____

____

____

If You Want to Go Deeper: *Tom Bennett's Running the Room is a clear, no-nonsense guide to classroom management that treats the work as a craft to be learned, not a talent to be born with. His writing is direct, practical, and honest.*

PART III:
INTERVENTION

Chapter 13
Do Not Let One Student Take Over the Class

One of the hardest lessons in classroom management is learning that you cannot let one student take the whole class away from everyone else.

That sounds obvious.

But in a real classroom, it is not always easy.

Sometimes one student pulls at you all period long through interruptions, arguing, refusal, side comments, attitude, or constant attempts to get a reaction. If you are not careful, that one student can end up taking most of your energy while the other students slowly lose access to their teacher.

That is a real problem.

Not because the student should be ignored.
Not because behavior does not need to be addressed.
But because the rest of the class needs you too.

A teacher has a responsibility to address behavior. But a teacher also has a responsibility to protect the learning, time, and stability of the whole room. If one student keeps pulling you into a battle, and you keep giving more and more of the period to that student, the class starts revolving around them.

That is not fair to everyone else.

And honestly, it usually does not help the student either.

I learned this clearly with a student I will call Joseph. He was in one of my most difficult classes, a group that was already loud, energetic, and hard to settle. He was an athlete, loud, and liked being the center of attention. He often tried to pull the focus of the room toward himself.

One day, I redirected him and told him clearly, "This is your first warning." He settled down for the moment.

But the next day, he came in with the same energy.

At that point, I knew I could not let the pattern continue. I also knew I did not want to spend the whole period going back and forth with him in front of everyone else. His behavior was disruptive, but it was not serious enough for the office. So I used another option.

I sent him next door to reset with my teammate and told him to come back during the last five minutes of class.

When he returned, we had a short conversation, and I asked him to complete a reflection. I wanted to address the behavior without letting it take over the class.

That experience stayed with me because it reminded me that sometimes a warning is not enough, but that does not mean the only next step is the office. If you have a good relationship with the teachers around you, sending a student to another classroom for a brief reset can be a very helpful option.

There was another day with Joseph that taught me something different.

The class was doing the warm-up when he suddenly became upset because he thought one of his friends had taken his pencil. I did not actually see what happened, but I could see that he was escalating quickly. He started raising his voice across the room, demanding that his friend give it back.

I told him to sit down and calm down. He told me what he believed had happened, and I asked the other student about it. The student looked genuinely surprised and said he had not taken the pencil. I told Joseph to take one from the pencil parking in the classroom, but he refused. He wanted his pencil, and he kept raising his voice at the other student.

I gave him a warning and told him he needed to calm down. He did not.

At that point, the situation was no longer just about a pencil. It was becoming disrespectful and aggressive, and it was starting to feel unsafe. I told him that if he could not calm down, he could not stay in the room. When he continued, I called for an administrator and asked for him to be removed for safety. I completed the referral and contacted his mother afterward.

That situation helped. I did not have another moment like that with him again, and over time his behavior improved.

The following year, I taught his sister, and she told me he had spoken well of me. That stayed with me because it reminded me that students do not always resent firm boundaries the way teachers fear they will. Many of them respond well to adults who are clear, consistent, and willing to hold the line without making things personal.

Not every behavior issue needs the office.

But that does not mean a student should be allowed to keep taking over the class.

Many times, when a student keeps pulling your attention during class, they are not looking for a long public lecture. They are looking for power, an audience, a delay, or a reaction.

That is why teachers have to choose their battles wisely.

Choosing your battles does not mean giving up.
It does not mean allowing disrespect.

It means asking better questions:

- Does this need my full attention right now?
- Does this need a quick redirection or a private conversation later?
- Does this student need a reset?
- Am I helping the room, or am I feeding a power struggle?

At the beginning, it is easy to feel like you have to fully address every challenge the moment it appears. It can feel like if you do not, you are losing control.

But sometimes the opposite is true.

Sometimes overreacting to one student gives away more control than a calm, brief response ever would.

That is why I believe teachers need to remember something simple:

You are the adult.

You are not another teenager in the argument.
You are not there to go back and forth.
You are not there to prove you can win a verbal fight.

The moment a teacher starts arguing emotionally, reacting personally, or matching a student's attitude, the room changes.

At that point, the teacher is no longer really leading.

The teacher is participating in the chaos.

And students can tell immediately.

One of the strongest things a teacher can do is refuse to become part of the performance.

A student may roll their eyes.
A student may mutter something under their breath.
A student may try to challenge you publicly.
A student may try to get the class watching.

You do not have to accept that invitation.

That is power.

Because real authority is not proving you can go back and forth with a child. Real authority is knowing you do not need to.

This does not mean being passive.
It does not mean ignoring serious behavior.

It means responding with intention instead of ego.

Students at this age often test adults by trying to pull them into emotional reactions. Sometimes they want attention. Sometimes they want control. Sometimes they want to perform for their peers.

And if the teacher reacts at the same level, the student often wins the moment.

Why?

Because the room is no longer centered on learning or structure.
It is centered on the conflict.

That is exactly what we do not want.

I have learned that some of the strongest classroom management is quiet:

- a brief redirection
- a calm consequence
- a reset in another classroom
- a private conversation later
- a quick note for documentation
- a refusal to argue in public
- a decision to keep teaching

That kind of response protects the whole class.

Because while one student may be trying to pull your attention, there are many others in the room watching. Some are ready to learn. Some are trying to stay focused. Some are waiting to see whether the room is still steady and still being led by an adult.

They need you too.

That is something teachers cannot forget.

I think many teachers, especially new teachers, feel that if they do not fully shut down every challenge in real time, they are failing. So they keep returning to the same student, the same exchange, and the same tension. Meanwhile, the rest of the room gets less instruction, less support, and less stability.

That is too expensive.

A teacher has to keep the whole room in view.

That is the real shift.

Not: How do I win against this one student?
But: How do I protect this classroom?

That question leads to better decisions.

Because once the goal becomes protecting the room, the teacher can think more clearly. They can respond without ego. They can keep the conflict from becoming the lesson. They can notice when a student needs less public attention and more private follow-through.

That is stronger classroom management.

And over time, students learn something important from that too.

They learn that one person cannot easily derail the room.
They learn that the teacher does not accept every invitation to conflict.
They learn that the class still moves forward.
They learn that the adult in the room is not controlled by whoever is loudest.

That is powerful.

Because classrooms feel safer when students know the room will not be handed over to one person's disruption.

I think that is one of the clearest signs of leadership.

The teacher addresses what needs to be addressed.
The teacher does not overreact.
The teacher protects the group.
The teacher follows up when needed.

Because one student may need support, correction, and consequences.

But the rest of the room still deserves stability, instruction, and a teacher who keeps leading.

What I Learned

I learned that if I gave one student too much of my time, attention, and emotion, the whole class paid the price. I still had to address behavior, but I also had to protect the room. The goal was not to win against one student. The goal was to keep leading the class.

Why This Works

Teachers make better decisions when they focus on protecting the whole classroom instead of getting pulled into one student's moment. Short, clear responses keep the lesson moving, reduce power struggles, and help the teacher hold boundaries without turning the conflict into the center of the class. When needed, a brief reset or a stronger consequence can interrupt the pattern and protect the room.

Try This Tomorrow

When one student starts pulling too much of your attention:

- keep your response short

- give the direction
- avoid arguing in public
- return to the lesson
- follow up later if needed
- escalate when safety requires it

Say less.

Protect the room.

My Next Move

When one student starts taking too much of the class, how can I respond in a way that protects everyone else without feeding the conflict?

____

____

____

____

If You Want to Go Deeper: *Tom Bennett's Running the Room offers one of the clearest explanations of how teachers can protect the learning environment without getting pulled into unnecessary conflict. It is especially useful for teachers who want to respond to disruption with more calm, brevity, and control instead of feeding public power struggles.*

Chapter 14
Delay the Referral and Stay in Control

One of the most important classroom management lessons I learned was this: not every problem needs an immediate referral.

That does not mean serious behavior should be ignored.
It does not mean teachers should tolerate chaos.
And it does not mean you should carry everything alone.

It means a referral should not be your first move for every difficult situation.

In the previous chapter, I shared an example of a student I called Joseph. Sometimes he needed a reset in another classroom. One time, I did need to call for an administrator because the situation had become aggressive and unsafe. The response depended on the moment.

At first, this was hard for me to figure out.

When behavior became frustrating, disruptive, or repeated, it was easy to think, *I need to send this student out. I need admin to handle this. I need this off my plate right now.*

And to be honest, sometimes that feeling came less from strategy and more from frustration

That is real.

When a student keeps interrupting, refusing, arguing, distracting others, or testing limits, teachers get tired. In that tiredness, a referral can start to feel like relief.

But relief and effectiveness are not always the same thing.

I had to learn that if I referred students too quickly, I sometimes skipped the real work of classroom management. I skipped the chance to reteach, redirect, document, contact home, change the environment, or respond with consistency. I moved to outside help before I had fully used the tools inside the classroom.

That weakens the room over time.

Students notice when a teacher sends problems away too quickly. They begin to see that the teacher's authority depends on removal instead of leadership. If removal becomes the main strategy, the classroom never really gets stronger. It just becomes dependent on the next rescue.

That is not sustainable.

So I learned to slow down.

Not passively.
Not permissively.
Deliberately.

Before writing a referral, I started asking myself harder questions:

- Have I clearly taught the expectation?

- Have I reminded the student privately?
- Have I followed through consistently?
- Have I tried a seat change, a reset, or a consequence?
- Have I contacted home if the behavior is becoming a pattern?
- Have I documented what is happening?
- Is this behavior truly beyond classroom management, or am I just at the end of my patience?

That last question requires honesty.

Sometimes teachers refer too soon not because the behavior is severe, but because it is repeated and emotionally draining.

But repeated does not automatically mean referral.

Sometimes it means the teacher needs a stronger response, a better intervention, or more consistency.

For example, at my school, repeated tardiness can lead to a referral. One day, I noticed a student who had been tardy five times in a single month. Instead of immediately writing the referral, I called her over and asked if everything was okay. She told me that on some mornings, the crowd of students outside overwhelmed her, and she had trouble getting herself through the door.

That conversation changed how I saw the situation.

The tardiness still needed to be addressed.
The expectation did not change.
But now I understood that the behavior was connected to
something more specific than simple carelessness.

That did not remove the expectation. It changed the way I responded.

I still had to address the pattern.

But I was no longer responding blindly.

That kind of clarity is important in classroom management because teachers need to know what they are actually responding to.

A teacher should be able to tell the difference between low-level disruption, repeated off-task behavior, open defiance, emotional escalation, and behavior that raises a safety concern.

Those are not all the same.

A student talking out of turn is not the same as threatening someone.
A student refusing to begin work is not the same as throwing a chair.
A student being annoying is not the same as a student being unsafe.

That sounds obvious, but stress can blur that line. When teachers are worn down, everything starts to feel bigger than it is.

That is why delay can be helpful.

It creates space to ask:

What is this, really?
Is this something I should handle in the classroom?
Is this a pattern I need to document and escalate properly?
Or is this already beyond what should remain in the room?

Teachers need to be able to tell the difference.

Because while I do not think teachers should refer too quickly, I also believe some things should not be delayed.

If a student is threatening someone, becoming physically aggressive, harassing another student, making the room unsafe, or escalating beyond classroom control, that is not the time to prove you can handle everything alone.

That is not strength.

That is poor judgment.

Delaying the referral does not mean delaying necessary support. It means do not outsource what is yours to manage, but also do not hold on to what is no longer yours to manage alone.

That is the balance.

Over time, I learned that the goal is not to avoid referrals completely. The goal is to use them wisely.

A good referral is specific, documented, and supported by prior steps when appropriate. It is not vague. It is not emotional. It is not written just because the teacher is fed up.

If I eventually need support from administration, I want to be able to say:

- this is the pattern
- these are the behaviors
- these are the steps I have already taken
- this is how often it has happened
- this is why classroom intervention is no longer enough

That is a stronger position.

It also helps administrators respond more effectively. A clear pattern is easier to support than a general statement like, "This student is always disrespectful," or "I cannot deal with this anymore."

Those feelings may be real, but they are not enough on their own.

I also learned that sometimes teachers use referrals to solve problems that are actually instructional or relational.

A student may be acting out because they do not understand the work.

A student may be avoiding it because they feel embarrassed.

A student may be escalating publicly because they do not want to look embarrassed in front of their peers.

A student may respond better to a private correction than a public one.

That does not mean every behavior has a hidden explanation. Sometimes a student is simply making a poor choice.

But if a teacher never pauses to examine the context, the response can become too simple:

Bad behavior. Write a referral. Remove student.

Sometimes that is appropriate.

Often it is not enough.

A better teacher question is this: *What is driving this behavior, and what response actually fits it?*

That question leads to better decisions. It keeps referrals from becoming lazy. It keeps teachers from escalating every repeated irritation. And it keeps teachers from pretending everything belongs in the classroom when it clearly does not.

Delay is not denial.

Delay is judgment.

And judgment is one of the most important parts of classroom management.

A teacher who refers too quickly may lose authority. A teacher who never refers may lose perspective. A teacher who knows when to hold, when to intervene, and when to escalate is usually stronger.

That kind of judgment helps the room feel stable. Students begin to see that consequences are predictable. They see that the teacher does not overreact to everything, but also does not ignore what matters.

That builds trust.

I also think delaying referrals forces teachers to strengthen their own systems. If you know you cannot immediately send every problem away, you become more aware of what your classroom is missing. Maybe the expectations are not clear enough. Maybe transitions are weak. Maybe follow-through is inconsistent. Maybe parent contact is happening too late. Maybe the student needs a more strategic seat. Maybe the teacher is reacting emotionally instead of instructionally.

Those are uncomfortable truths sometimes, but they are useful ones.

Because the goal is not just to survive each bad moment. The goal is to build a classroom where fewer things need to become office problems in the first place.

That is real classroom management.

Still, I want to say this clearly: there is no prize for handling too much alone.

If you have tried reasonable classroom interventions, documented the pattern, contacted home when appropriate, and the behavior continues in a way that damages learning or safety, then escalation is not weakness.

It is the next step.

Teachers should not refer every problem too soon. But they also should not delay support so long that the classroom suffers unnecessarily.

The room matters.
The other students matter.
Your capacity matters too.

Sometimes teachers become so determined not to "give up" on a student that they allow one student to consume too much time, energy, and attention.

That is not fair to anyone.

So yes, delay the referral.

But do it with purpose.

Delay long enough to teach, intervene, document, communicate, and think clearly. Delay long enough to make sure the response fits the behavior. Delay long enough to lead the room instead of managing from frustration.

But do not delay so long that the classroom pays the price for your hesitation.

That is the line.

If I could say it simply, I would say this:

A referral should not be your first move, and it should not be your forbidden move. It should be your right move when classroom management has been used well and is no longer enough.

That is what I had to learn.

And once I learned it, I became more thoughtful, more consistent, and more effective.

Not because student behavior got easy.

But because my judgment got stronger.

What I Learned

I learned that sending students out too quickly can weaken the classroom. A referral has its place, but it should usually come after I have tried to address the situation in the classroom, unless the behavior is serious or unsafe. The goal is not to avoid referrals. The goal is to use them with judgment.

Why This Works

When teachers do not rush to referrals, they have more space to reteach, intervene, document, and communicate. That helps them strengthen the classroom and make better decisions about when a situation really needs to be escalated. It also helps the room feel more stable and gives referrals more weight when they are needed.

Try This Tomorrow

Before writing your next referral, pause and ask:

- Have I addressed this clearly?
- Have I followed through?
- Have I documented the pattern?
- Does this need classroom intervention or administrative support?

Do not refer from frustration.

Refer from judgment.

My Next Move

Am I handling referrals with good judgment, or am I responding too quickly in some moments and waiting too long in others?

____

____

____

____

If You Want to Go Deeper: *Ross Greene's Lost at School is especially helpful for teachers trying to understand challenging behavior before rushing to punishment or removal. His work encourages adults to look beneath behavior, identify lagging skills, and respond with more thoughtful intervention.*

Chapter 15
Make Parent Contact Work for You

One of the most useful things I learned about classroom management was this: parent contact works better when it is clear, respectful, and timely.

It also works better when it does not begin only when everything is already falling apart.

At first, contacting parents about behavior felt intimidating. I did not always know when to reach out, what to say, or how direct to be. I think a lot of new teachers struggle with that. Some avoid parent contact for too long because they do not want conflict. Others wait until they are already frustrated and then write with too much emotion behind the message.

Neither one helps.

During my first year, I did not really know how to contact parents about behavior, so I asked a coworker for help. She told me I needed to be firm in my email and say that if the student did not improve, the next step would be a referral. She even shared a template with me that I could adjust and use.

At first, I followed that advice.

Some parents responded very briefly, almost coldly, with messages like, "Ok, thanks." Some never responded at all. One time, I got an email from a mother that made me feel like she thought I was lying. She basically said her son would never do that and questioned why I was already talking about a referral.

That made me pause.

I started asking myself whether the email itself was part of the problem. I also thought about it as a parent. If I received a message like that about my own child, how would I feel? And honestly, especially at the beginning when I preferred emailing over calling because I was nervous, I realized those messages sounded more like warnings than communication.

That was a turning point for me.

I realized the email was missing warmth. It was missing humanity. So I changed my approach. I started including something positive and true about the student. Even when a child was difficult, there was always something honest I could say. I also stopped using the word referral unless it was truly necessary, because many times, after contacting home and building a partnership with the parent, I no longer needed to take that step.

Over time, I learned that parent communication does not need to be dramatic to be effective. In fact, it usually works better when it is calm, brief, and focused on support.

My goal is not to shame the student.
My goal is not to prove that I am right.
My goal is not to dump frustration onto a parent.

My goal is to communicate clearly, document what is happening, build a partnership with parents, and invite support before the problem gets bigger.

That change made my communication more effective and my classroom easier to manage.

One experience helped confirm that for me. I had a student who was failing and constantly off task. When I emailed her father, I began with something honest and positive about his daughter. I told him she was smart, that she participated when she was focused, and that I believed she could do better. Then I clearly described the pattern I was seeing: missing work, repeated redirection, and a declining grade. I did not mention a referral because it was not necessary, and in the end, it was not needed.

Her father responded within the hour.

He thanked me for seeing his daughter as more than a problem. He said most emails from school made him feel defensive. That one conversation changed the dynamic completely.

The student improved over the next two weeks.

Not because one email fixed everything.
But because the father felt respected, and that opened the door to real partnership.

That experience reinforced something I had already started to learn: it is not only what you say. It is how you say it.

A parent should be able to hear concern without feeling like the email is just a threat in nicer clothes.

That is why I try to write with care. I want parents to know that their child matters to me, even when I am reaching out about a problem. I want the message to feel like support, not punishment.

That also means beginning with something positive that is real, not forced.

Even the most challenging student usually has something honest and positive you can say. Maybe they are bright. Maybe they are funny. Maybe they are trying more than it looks. The point is to say something true.

Then I move into the concern clearly.

I say what I have noticed.
I describe the behavior factually.
I explain what I have already done.
I ask for support.

That is the structure I come back to again and again.

I do not exaggerate.
I do not write while angry.
And I do not make the email longer than it needs to be.

A behavior email should not read like an essay. It should sound calm, clear, and professional. Parents need to understand what happened, what has already been tried, and what support is being requested.

So instead of saying a student is disrespectful all the time, I try to describe what I actually saw:

- talking during instruction
- refusing to move seats
- repeated tardiness

- calling out after reminders
- continuing to distract others after redirection

That kind of language is more useful because it keeps the focus on behavior instead of emotion.

I also think it is important to say what I have already done before contacting home.

That might include:

- reviewing expectations
- giving reminders
- redirecting privately
- changing a seat
- giving a warning
- following a classroom consequence

When parents can see that I already tried to handle the issue in class, the message feels more balanced and professional. It shows that I am not reaching out over one small thing without first doing my part.

This is especially important in Grades 6–9.

Not every poor choice needs immediate parent contact. But repeated behavior, refusal, patterns, or problems that are not improving after classroom intervention often do.

A parent email can create accountability, lead to an important conversation at home, and help the student realize the behavior is being noticed. It can also create a record if more support is needed later.

That is one reason I do not believe in waiting too long. If a behavior is becoming a pattern, reaching out early is usually better than waiting until I am already overwhelmed.

It also helps when the message is written as a partnership, not an attack.

I might say:

"I would appreciate your support in talking with your child about this."
"I want to work together to help them be successful in class."
"Please let me know if there is anything I should be aware of that may be affecting them at school."

That kind of language invites cooperation.

Not every parent will respond. Not every parent will agree. Not every message will lead to immediate change.

But that does not make the communication useless.

It keeps families informed. It shows professionalism. And it strengthens your next step if the behavior continues.

That leads to another important point: documentation.

Any time I contact home about behavior, I document it:

- when I contacted
- who I contacted
- what the concern was
- how I contacted them
- whether they responded

- any next steps

That protects you. It helps you stay organized, and it is important if you eventually need support from a counselor, administrator, or behavior team.

But parent communication should not exist only when there is a problem.

That is another lesson I learned.

Positive emails matter too.

If families only ever hear from you when their child is off task, disrespectful, or struggling, then every message from you starts to feel negative before they even open it. But when families sometimes hear good news too, trust grows.

A short positive email can go a long way.

It does not need to be long.
It does not need to be polished.
It just needs to be genuine and specific.

If a student shows improvement, kindness, effort, leadership, responsibility, or growth, that is worth communicating.

Those messages help because they remind families that I notice more than problems. They also build a stronger relationship before I ever need to contact home about something difficult.

I also think regular communication helps. I try to send a newsletter every two or three weeks so families know what is happening in class. I include upcoming tests, what we are covering, what is coming next, tutoring days, and where to check for missing assignments.

Parents really value that kind of communication, and it helps build partnership before there is ever a problem.

One thing I would tell any new teacher is this: do not wait until you are emotionally drained to contact home. Write before you are at your limit—while you can still be clear, factual, calm, and professional. That alone can change the outcome.

Parent contact should sound like communication, not a threat.

The email is not the consequence. It is a tool.

It brings another adult into the conversation.
It supports the student.
It makes expectations visible beyond the classroom.
And it helps the teacher avoid carrying everything alone.

Used well, it can be one of the most effective classroom management tools you have.

Not because it is forceful.
But because it is clear, respectful, timely, and rooted in care.

What I Learned

I learned that parent contact works best when it is respectful, specific, and timely. Waiting too long usually makes the message more emotional and less effective. When I communicate clearly and invite support, parent contact becomes a tool for problem-solving instead of just a reaction to frustration.

Why This Works

Parent contact is more effective when families feel informed, respected, and included instead of blamed. Clear communication builds accountability, creates a record, and often brings support before a behavior problem gets bigger.

Try This Tomorrow

If one student's behavior is becoming a pattern, send one clear, calm message home.

Keep it simple:

- start with one honest positive
- name the behavior clearly
- say what you have already done
- ask for support

Write to communicate, not to vent.

My Next Move

Am I contacting parents early enough for the communication to be helpful, or am I waiting until I am already frustrated?

____

____

____

____

If You Want to Go Deeper: *Doug Lemov's Teach Like a Champion offers helpful ideas about communication, expectations, and how adult responses shape student behavior. For parent communication specifically, the most important* *principle is not having the perfect script. It is learning how to be clear, respectful, specific, and timely. Parents are more likely to respond well when they feel informed instead of blamed, and that kind of communication gets stronger with practice.*

Chapter 16
Know When Your Strategies Aren't Enough

One of the hardest things I had to learn as a teacher was this: not every behavior problem can be solved with good classroom management alone.

That was an important lesson for me, because at first I put too much pressure on myself. If a student kept struggling, I immediately wondered what I was doing wrong. I asked myself whether I had not been clear enough, consistent enough, calm enough, or strong enough.

Sometimes that kind of reflection is useful.
Teachers should reflect.

But sometimes the truth is simpler: some situations are bigger than what one teacher can fix inside one classroom.

That is important to remember.

If you believe every difficult behavior is your fault, you will carry too much. You will start blaming yourself for things that require a bigger team, more support, and resources beyond your room.

That was a necessary lesson for me, because at first I put too much pressure on myself. If a student kept struggling, I immediately wondered what I was doing wrong. I asked myself whether I had not been clear enough, consistent enough, calm enough, or firm enough.

Sometimes that kind of reflection is useful.
Teachers should reflect.

But sometimes the truth is simpler: some situations are bigger than what one teacher can fix inside one classroom.

That matters.

If you believe every difficult behavior is your fault, you will carry too much. You will start blaming yourself for things that require a bigger team, more help, and resources beyond your room.

Classroom management matters.
Relationships matter.
Clear expectations matter.
Follow-through matters.

But even when those things are in place, some students still need more.

That does not mean your classroom system is weak.
It does not mean you failed.
It means classroom management has limits.

Teachers need to know that.

Some students are dealing with anxiety, trauma, family instability, emotional regulation issues, mental health struggles, academic frustration, or patterns of behavior that go beyond what a warning, a consequence, a parent email, or a seat change can solve.

You may still need to respond.
You may still need to hold boundaries.
You may still need to document and follow through.

But you also need to recognize when the problem is no longer only about classroom management.

That recognition changes the next step.

Instead of asking, *How do I control this better?* sometimes the better question is, *Who else needs to be involved so this student gets the support they need?*

That is a healthier mindset.

One of the most important parts of growing as a teacher was learning to tell the difference between a student who needed correction and a student who needed more support than I could provide by myself.

Sometimes that difference was obvious.
Sometimes it was not.

Sometimes I had already redirected, assigned consequences, contacted home, documented the pattern, and stayed consistent, and still nothing changed. The student was not just off task or defiant. They were overwhelmed, shut down, explosive, emotionally unreachable, or escalating beyond what normal classroom responses could handle.

Those moments taught me something clear: not every behavior problem is solved by being stricter.

That does not mean consequences do not matter.
They do.

But consequences alone cannot solve every problem.

A student who is dysregulated may need more than correction.
A student carrying a lot from home may need more than a warning.
A student with repeated emotional outbursts may need more than a referral.
A student who keeps shutting down may need more than "try harder."

That is when teachers need support too.

During my second year, I had a student I will call Nina. She was very sweet, but she was hard to reach academically. During group work, Nina often chose talking with classmates over getting the assignment done. Over time, that pattern affected her grade, and she was failing my class.

I tried contacting home. I wanted to reach her mother first, but there was no contact information listed for her. The only parent information in the system was for her father, so I contacted him instead several times and explained the situation, but he never responded. After multiple attempts, I still felt frustrated and unsure of what else to do, so I brought the situation to my academic dean for support.

That was when I learned her mother was in jail.

I went silent.

In that moment, my frustration shifted. I realized I had been looking at her behavior without fully understanding what she might have been carrying outside of school.

After that, I started building a real connection with her. I greeted her every day. I asked about her weekend. I tried to notice her beyond the gradebook.

She began to change.

She started turning in work.
She started opening up more.
She started hugging me when she came into class.

She still failed that year. By the time I truly reached her, too much time had already passed.

But she did not leave feeling invisible.

That experience taught me something I still carry with me: before we decide who a student is, we need to remember how much we may not know.

I think this is especially important for new teachers to hear, because many believe that if they were better at classroom management, every student would respond.

That is simply not true.

Good classroom management can prevent a lot.
It can reduce chaos.
It can create safety.
It can improve behavior.
It can protect learning.

But it cannot erase every deeper issue a student brings into the room.

Teachers should not be expected to carry that unrealistic burden.

Sometimes the most professional thing you can do is recognize that a student needs a bigger team.

That might mean involving:

- an administrator

- a counselor
- a social worker
- a case manager
- a behavior specialist
- a parent or guardian
- another teacher who sees the same student
- a school support team

The exact structure depends on the school.

But the principle is the same: when a pattern continues beyond your classroom interventions, do not keep carrying it alone just because you think asking for help means you failed.

It does not.

In fact, asking for help at the right time is part of doing your job well.

I had to learn that.

Strong teachers are not the ones who try to handle everything alone forever. They are the ones who know when to keep working the plan, when to document, and when to say, "This student needs more support than I can give by myself."

That is wisdom, not weakness.

It is also important because students deserve more than one exhausted adult trying to hold everything together alone.

That truth brings relief.

It also helps prevent burnout.

Teachers burn out faster when they believe every difficult student is a personal failure. That mindset creates guilt, pressure, and emotional exhaustion. But when teachers understand that some situations require a team, they can stay more grounded. They can keep doing their part without trying to be everything for everyone.

That does not make us less caring.
It makes us more sustainable.

And sustainability is necessary in this profession.

I also think students benefit when teachers are honest about their limits.

Not cold.
Not careless.
Honest.

Because when we are honest, we are more likely to ask for the right help. And when we ask for the right help, students are more likely to get what they actually need.

That is better for everyone.

The truth is, classroom management can do a lot. It can create structure, protect learning, reduce chaos, and solve many everyday problems before they grow.

But it cannot solve every deep need, every emotional wound, every crisis, or every long-term pattern by itself.

Sometimes what a student needs is not more control.

Sometimes what they need is more support.

And part of becoming a strong teacher is learning the difference.

This is also where professional judgment matters.

A student talking too much, testing boundaries, or refusing small directions may still be within the teacher's lane. That is often classroom management.

But a student who is repeatedly dysregulated, emotionally shut down, aggressive, unsafe, self-destructive, or clearly unraveling may be showing you something bigger.

That is not the moment to keep asking, *What consequence should I try next?*

That is the moment to step back and ask:

- What pattern am I seeing?
- What have I already tried?
- What is not changing?
- Who else needs to know this?

Those are the right questions.

Because the longer teachers try to solve bigger problems with only classroom tools, the more frustrated they become. And the more frustrated they become, the more likely they are to either overreact or lose hope.

Neither one helps.

That is why documentation matters here too.

If I think a student needs more support, I want to be able to explain why clearly.

Not:

"He is always a problem."
"She never listens."
"I cannot deal with this anymore."

Even if that is how I feel, that language is too vague to help.

What helps is clarity:

- What behaviors are happening?
- How often?
- What interventions have already been tried?
- What parent contact has happened?
- What changes have you noticed?
- What makes you believe this is bigger than classroom correction?

That is the kind of information that gets taken seriously.

It also protects you.

Because if a student truly needs more support, vague frustration is not enough. You need a clear picture. And the clearer that picture is, the easier it is for the next person—counselor, administrator, support staff, or family—to step in effectively.

I also learned that not every struggling student looks the same.

Some are loud.
Some are oppositional.
Some are disruptive.
Some are angry.

But others struggle quietly.
Some disappear into silence.
Some stop turning in work.
Some shut down.
Some avoid eye contact.
Some hide behind indifference.

Teachers have to notice that.

If we only pay attention to the students who are hard to manage publicly, we may miss the students who are hurting privately.

Those students need support too.

That is why this chapter is not only about behavior. It is also about recognition.

We have to notice patterns.
We have to pay attention.
We have to stop assuming that every struggling student simply needs firmer discipline.

Sometimes they do need discipline.

Sometimes they need something more.

A strong teacher learns not to confuse the two.

I do not want teachers reading this book to come away thinking classroom management is powerless.

It is not.

Good classroom management solves many problems before they become bigger ones. It gives students structure, predictability, and safety. It helps prevent escalation. It protects learning for everyone else in the room.

That is real.

But I also do not want teachers believing that if something is not improving, they just need to work harder, be stricter, or keep carrying more.

That is not always true.

Sometimes what a student needs is not more control.

What they need is more support.

The right next step is not always more classroom pressure.

It may be a conversation with a counselor.
It may be an administrator.
It may be a case manager.
It may be a family meeting.
Sometimes it is simply telling the truth: this student is not responding to classroom intervention alone.

And part of becoming a strong teacher is learning the difference.

That is not giving up on a student.

It is refusing to pretend that one teacher can do the work of an entire team.

That distinction matters.

One of the fastest ways teachers burn out is by confusing care with over-responsibility.

You can care deeply about a student and still need help.
You can do your job well and still need support.
You can be consistent, prepared, warm, and professional and still have students whose needs go beyond what you can solve alone.

That does not make you ineffective.

It makes you honest.

And honest teachers usually make better decisions than teachers who try to look invincible.

If I could say it simply, I would say this:

Classroom management is powerful, but it is not all-powerful.

It can do a lot.
It cannot do everything.

Once I understood that, I became a better teacher.

Not because the hard situations disappeared.
But because I stopped taking every hard situation as proof that I had failed.

I learned to do my part well. I learned to document clearly. I learned to ask for help sooner. And I learned that some students do not need a stronger teacher voice. They need a stronger support system around them.

That is one of the clearest lessons I have learned in this work.

What I Learned

I learned that not every behavior problem can be solved by classroom management alone. Some students need more support than one teacher can provide. Once I understood that, I stopped blaming myself for every hard situation and started making better decisions about when to ask for help.

Why This Works

Teachers are more effective when they know the difference between a problem that can be addressed through classroom management and a problem that needs a wider support system. That keeps teachers from carrying too much alone, and it helps students get the kind of support that actually fits the situation.

Try This Tomorrow

Think of one student whose behavior or disengagement has not improved despite your usual classroom strategies.

Ask yourself:

- What have I already tried?
- What pattern am I seeing?
- Is this still a classroom issue, or does this student need more support?
- Who else needs to know?

Do not assume you have to solve everything alone.

My Next Move

Is there a student I keep trying to manage alone when what they really need is a stronger support system?

____

____

____

If You Want to Go Deeper: *Ross Greene's Lost at School offers one of the most helpful frameworks for understanding student behavior that goes beyond typical classroom management. His Collaborative and Proactive Solutions approach is especially useful when a student's needs clearly require more than consequences alone.*

PART IV:
RESET

Chapter 17
Reset the Room Without Starting Over

One of the most important things I have learned about classroom management is this: not every bad moment has to become a bad day.

That may sound obvious, but many teachers do not really know how to live it out.

A class goes badly.
A student pushes every limit.
You lose patience.
The room feels tense.
The lesson falls apart.

And suddenly, it is easy to feel like everything is off now.

I know that feeling. There have been days when I left class replaying everything in my head—thinking about what I should have said differently, what I should have done earlier, or why the whole period felt harder than it should have. Sometimes it was one student. Sometimes it was the whole class. Sometimes it was just one of those days when I was tired, they were restless, and everything seemed to go wrong at once.

Those days happen.

And when they do, one of the most important skills a teacher can develop is knowing how to reset.

Not ignore.
Not pretend nothing happened.
Not lower expectations.

Reset.

A reset means I do not let one hard moment define the next class period, the rest of the week, or the whole relationship with a student. It means I deal with what needs to be dealt with, but I also create a way forward.

That became very important for me because if you do not know how to reset, you start carrying too much. You bring yesterday's frustration into today's lesson. You walk into the room already tense. You start expecting the worst before students even do anything.

And students feel that.

They notice when a teacher is still irritated.
They notice when the room feels heavy.
They notice when one bad day changes the whole tone of the class.

Sometimes the reset is mostly internal. It is taking a breath before the next class comes in. It is refusing to replay the same moment all day. It is reminding yourself that one rough lesson does not mean you are a bad teacher. It is choosing not to teach from frustration the next day.

Other times, the reset needs to happen with students too.

Maybe the class was too loud.
Maybe transitions were messy.
Maybe students were disrespectful.
Maybe one student crossed a line.
Maybe the room just felt chaotic and off.

In those moments, I do not think the answer is to act like nothing happened. But I also do not think the answer is to keep teaching from a place of anger. What works better is naming the issue clearly, briefly, and calmly, then moving forward with a plan.

That might sound like this:

"Yesterday did not go the way it needed to go. We are resetting today. This is what needs to be different. This is what I expect from you. And this is how we are going to start again."

That kind of language is direct without being dramatic. It tells students three things:

- I noticed.
- It needs to change.
- We are moving forward.

That is strong classroom leadership.

I think some teachers hesitate to reset because they think it makes them look weak. They think if they are not still visibly upset, students will assume the behavior did not matter.

I do not agree.

Resetting is not weakness.
It is leadership.

It takes maturity to correct a problem without making it the emotional center of the classroom for days. It takes professionalism to address what happened, reteach what needs to be retaught, and come back steady the next day.

Students need that. At this age, they have a lot of bad moments. They are impulsive. They are emotional. They make poor choices in front of peers. They say things the wrong way. They react before they think.

If a teacher treats every bad moment like a permanent label, the relationship starts to break down quickly.

That is why I believe students need a real chance to recover.

That does not remove accountability or consequences. It means a student should know that one bad day does not have to become a permanent identity in your room.

I feel strongly about that. Many students already walk around feeling like they are the difficult one, the disrespectful one, or the problem student. I do not want my classroom to reinforce that more than it already has to. I want students to know that behavior matters, choices matter, and consequences matter. But I also want them to know they can come back from a bad moment.

That is part of a healthy classroom.

I also think teachers need to give themselves that same chance.

Some days you will not respond perfectly.
Some days your tone will be sharper than you wanted.
Some days you will realize later that you should have handled something differently.

That does not automatically mean you are failing. It means you are teaching human beings while also being a human being.

The goal is not perfection.
The goal is reflection.

After a hard day, I try to ask myself a few honest questions:

- What actually happened?
- What triggered the problem?
- What part belonged to the students?
- What part belonged to me?
- What needs to be retaught?
- What needs a consequence?
- What just needs a fresh start?

Those questions help me reset with judgment instead of emotion.

Because not every bad day needs the same response.

Sometimes the class needs a reteach.
Sometimes a few students need private conversations.
Sometimes I need to tighten a routine.
Sometimes I need to change seats.
Sometimes I need to contact home.
Sometimes I need support.
And sometimes I simply need to come back calmer and more prepared the next day.

Sometimes a teacher reset has to be bigger than one deep breath between classes. Sometimes it means taking the personal day you need without guilt. Rest does not make you less committed, and it does not make you less effective. You are not a machine. If your classroom is built on clear routines and consistent expectations, one day away does not erase that work.

Sometimes the reset is rest.

That is why resetting is not the same as doing nothing.

A real reset still has structure behind it. It might mean:

- reteaching a procedure
- reviewing expectations
- assigning seats differently
- having a private conversation
- apologizing if your own response was not your best
- restarting class with a different opening
- slowing things down and rebuilding order

Those are active choices.

What I do not want teachers to believe is that they only have two options: either stay angry or act like nothing happened.

There is a better option.

Reset with purpose.

I have also learned that the first few minutes after a reset shape a lot. Tone matters. The opening matters. Body language matters. So does how much you say.

If I am trying to reset a class, I do not want to begin with a long lecture full of frustration. That usually makes things worse. Students stop listening, the mood gets heavier, and the class starts from a negative place.

Short and clear is better.

Something like this is usually enough:

"Yesterday we struggled with staying focused during instruction. That cannot continue. Today we are resetting. I am expecting better choices, and we are going to start with that right now."

That says enough.

Then I move into action.

Because a reset should not live only in words. It should show up in what happens next.

Maybe I tighten the entry routine.
Maybe I change the warm-up.
Maybe I review transitions.
Maybe I greet students at the door more intentionally.
Maybe I structure the period more tightly than I did before.

That is what makes the reset real.

I also think individual resets matter just as much as whole-class resets.

A student may have had a bad interaction with you yesterday. Maybe they were disrespectful. Maybe they shut down. Maybe you corrected them several times. Maybe both of you ended class frustrated.

The next day matters.

That next interaction can either help repair the relationship or make the tension worse. So after the issue has been handled, I try not to greet that student with yesterday still written all over my face. I do not want my expression, tone, or body language to say, *I am still holding this against you.*

Instead, I want the student to feel this:

What happened mattered.
We addressed it.
Now you have a chance to do better today.

That kind of reset can change a lot.

I had a student once who I will call Tim. He had a terrible day in my class—disruptive, argumentative, and shut down by the end of the period. I handled it professionally, documented it, and contacted home. But the next morning, I made a choice. When Tim walked in, I greeted him the same way I greeted everyone else. I did not bring up the day before. I did not give him a look that said I was still carrying it.

He paused for a second, almost surprised.

Then he sat down and started his warm-up.

That day was completely different.

Not because the reset erased the consequence. That had already happened. But the reset told him something important: yesterday is over. Today is a new chance.

Many students expect adults to stay angry. They expect adults to hold grudges, bring up old mistakes, or treat them like a problem before they even do anything. When a teacher stays firm but still allows a fresh start, students notice that too.

It builds credibility.

It shows them that your consequences are real, but your emotions are not running the room.

Resetting also protects teachers from burnout. If you never let go of bad moments, this job gets heavy fast. You cannot carry every rude comment, every failed lesson, every chaotic class, and every frustrating interaction as if it is permanent.

If you do, you will wear yourself down.

Part of surviving teaching is learning what deserves reflection and what you need to let go of at the end of the day.

That is especially important for new teachers. New teachers often think every hard day means they are not cut out for the job. I wish more of them knew this: a hard day is just a hard day.

It is data.
It is feedback.
It is a chance to adjust.
It is not always proof that everything is falling apart.

Sometimes the best thing you can do after a bad day is come back tomorrow with a calmer tone, a clearer plan, and less emotion.

Not because what happened did not matter.
But because the next day still deserves your best.

A classroom cannot function well if every mistake keeps defining what happens next.
And neither can a teacher.

If I could say it simply, I would say this:

- A reset is not pretending.

- A reset is not quitting.
- A reset is not lowering the bar.
- A reset is choosing to address what happened and still move forward with clarity, steadiness, and purpose.

That is one of the healthiest things a teacher can learn to do.

What I Learned

A bad class, a bad moment, or a bad day does not have to define what happens next. Strong classroom management includes knowing how to reset with clarity, hold accountability, and start again.

Why This Works

A reset helps teachers respond with judgment instead of emotion. It keeps frustration from spilling into the next class, protects relationships with students, and helps the room recover faster after a hard day.

Try This Tomorrow

If a class or a student had a rough day, do not walk in carrying yesterday's frustration.

Instead:

- name the issue briefly
- restate the expectation
- adjust one structure if needed
- start the class with a calm, clear tone

Reset on purpose.

My Next Move

After a hard day, do I know how to reset the room, or am I carrying the tension forward and letting it shape what happens next?

____

____

____

____

If You Want to Go Deeper: *Doug Lemov's Teach Like a Champion offers practical strategies for resetting expectations, tightening routines, and reestablishing control without turning the classroom into a lecture or a power struggle. It is especially helpful for teachers who want concrete ways to reset a class quickly, clearly, and with purpose after things start slipping.*

PART V: SUSTAINABILITY

Chapter 18
Protect Your Peace After School

One of the most damaging habits I developed as a teacher was letting the job follow me home.

I do not just mean papers, lesson plans, or emails.

I mean the mental weight of it.

I would leave the building, but the job would keep going in my head. I would replay student behavior, second-guess conversations, worry about what I forgot, think about what tomorrow might bring, and carry the emotional residue of the day into my evening.

That kind of carrying becomes normal if you are not careful.

In my first year, I was the teacher who brought everything home—stacks of papers, unfinished grading, unresolved stress. I thought that was what committed teachers did. I thought being a good teacher meant always doing more, always staying later, and always giving up more of myself.

The problem was that what I carried home was not just work.

I was also carrying exhaustion, guilt, and the feeling that I could never really be done.

And that cost me.

I was spending time correcting papers while my family was right there. I was home, but not really home. My attention was split. My body was in the room, but my mind was still at school.

Over time, I had to face something hard: I was giving school energy that belonged to my family.

That realization changed me.

I am not going to pretend I never brought work home again. That would not be honest. But I became much more intentional. I especially worked hard not to bring home grading.

That was a boundary I needed.

And once I started protecting my evenings more, I saw something clearly: it did not make me less committed. It made me more present at home and more rested at school.

The two were connected in ways I had not understood before.

Once taking the job home becomes normal, it starts draining you in ways you do not always notice right away.

You feel tired all the time.
You stop fully resting.
You lose patience faster.
You start Sunday already stressed about Monday.
You sit down at home, but your mind is still in your classroom.

That is not sustainable.

Teaching is demanding enough during the school day. If the job also takes over your nights, your weekends, your peace, and your inner life, it will wear you down much faster than it should.

I think many teachers are taught to expect this.

They are told the first years are hard.
They are told exhaustion is normal.
They are told caring deeply means thinking about students all the time.
They are told good teachers always do more.

Some of that messaging is dangerous.

If you are not careful, you start equating dedication with constant emotional availability. You start thinking that if you really care, you should always be thinking about the students, the lessons, the parent emails, the classroom problems, and the work still undone.

That belief will burn you out.

Caring about your students does not require carrying them mentally every hour of the day.

You can be committed without being consumed.
You can be responsible without being available to the job at all times.
You can care deeply and still decide that school does not get your whole evening.

That is not selfish.

It is necessary.

I had to learn that the hard way.

There were times when I thought I was being a better teacher because I kept thinking about everything after work. I thought the constant mental replay meant I was reflective, invested, and serious about getting better.

Sometimes reflection is useful.

But constant replay is not reflection.

Sometimes it is just stress repeating itself.

And stress does not automatically make you better.

In fact, when teachers never mentally leave the job, they often become less effective. They arrive already tired. They become emotionally thinner. Small problems feel bigger because there is no real recovery between school days.

Protecting your peace is not a soft idea.

It is a professional one.

If you want to last in this work, you need recovery.

Not fake recovery.
Not sitting on the couch while your mind is still at school.
Real recovery.

That means there have to be parts of your day where you are not teaching in your head.

For some teachers, the job follows them home because of workload. That is real. There is planning, grading, email, documentation, and all the unfinished things a school day does not always leave time for.

But for many teachers, the heavier problem is not just the tasks.

It is the emotional carryover.

A difficult parent message stays with you.
A student's disrespect stays with you.
A lesson that failed stays with you.

A child you are worried about stays with you.
A conversation with administration stays with you.

And if you do not learn how to set emotional boundaries, every day starts piling on top of the last one.

That pile gets heavy fast.

I am not saying teachers should become detached or cold.

I am saying teachers need boundaries strong enough to protect their energy and keep them from burning out.

There is a difference.

A healthy boundary sounds like this:

- I care about my students, but I cannot mentally relive every problem all night.
- I want to improve, but I am not going to analyze every mistake for three hours.
- I will do what needs to be done, but I will not let the job occupy every corner of my life.

Those are good boundaries.

And many teachers need permission to build them.

Because schools do not always teach this well.

Sometimes the culture rewards overextension. The teacher who answers emails late at night gets praised for being dedicated. The teacher who never stops working gets treated like the standard. The teacher who is exhausted but still saying yes to everything looks admirable from the outside.

But exhaustion is not professionalism.

And being constantly depleted is not proof that you care more.

It may just mean your boundaries are weak.

That was hard for me to admit.

Sometimes I was tired not only because teaching was hard, but because I had not learned how to stop the job from expanding into every available space.

School will take as much of you as you keep offering without limits.

If you do not decide where the line is, the line keeps moving.

There will always be more to do.

Another paper to grade.
Another lesson to improve.
Another email to answer.
Another student to worry about.
Another problem to revisit.

If your peace depends on finishing everything, you will almost never feel done.

Teachers need a different standard.

Not, *Is everything finished?*
But, *Have I done enough for today to stop?*

That question changed something for me.

Because enough is realistic.

Finished is often not.

There are days when enough looks like this:

- planning tomorrow's lesson
- answering the most important email
- grading what truly needs grading
- documenting the issue that cannot wait
- leaving the rest for tomorrow

That is not laziness.
That is triage.

And teachers who do not learn triage often drown in unnecessary guilt.

I also had to learn that not every thought needs to come home with me.

Some thoughts are useful:

- I need to reteach that routine tomorrow.
- I should call that parent.
- I need a better transition for my third period.
- That student may need support beyond my classroom.

Those thoughts can lead to action.

But many thoughts are not helping:

- Why did I say it that way?
- I am terrible at this.
- That class hates me.

- I should have done everything differently.
- I cannot stop thinking about what happened in my fifth period.

That kind of thinking does not improve tomorrow.

It just steals tonight.

And teachers need to know the difference.

Protecting your peace also means being careful about what you say yes to.

This profession can fill every extra inch of time if you let it.

Extra committees.
Extra roles.
Extra events.
Extra duties.
Extra emotional labor.
Extra unpaid time.

Sometimes saying yes is appropriate.

But if you are already struggling to stay grounded, saying yes to everything does not make you a team player.

It makes you easier to overload.

Teachers need to know when to help and when to protect their capacity.

That is not selfish.

That is survival.

I also think teachers need a way to end the day on purpose.

Not just physically leave.

End it.

That might mean making a short list for tomorrow before you go. It might mean clearing one surface, closing your laptop, shutting your classroom door, or deciding on one sentence in your head:

I did what I could today. The rest will wait.

That kind of closure helps more than people realize.

Without closure, the day follows you.
With closure, your brain has a better chance of letting go.

I am not pretending this is easy.

Some days stay with you because something really hard happened. Some students do weigh on you. Some problems do not fit neatly into contract hours. Teaching is personal work, and pretending otherwise would be dishonest.

But even then, teachers need limits.

You cannot be fully present for students if you are chronically depleted.
You cannot be patient if you never recover.
You cannot be clear-headed if your nervous system never settles down.
You cannot last if school lives in your body all the time.

Protecting your peace is part of protecting your teaching.

The calmer, steadier, more rested version of you is not less committed.

That version of you is more useful.

I wish more teachers heard that early.

Especially new teachers.

New teachers often believe that the more overwhelmed they are, the more seriously they are taking the job. They think constant worry means they are trying hard enough. They think boundaries are something you earn later, after proving yourself.

I do not think that is wise.

By the time many teachers realize they need boundaries, they are already exhausted, discouraged, or thinking about leaving.

That is too late.

Boundaries should not be the reward for surviving teaching.

They are part of how you survive it.

I also learned that peace does not always come from having fewer problems.

Sometimes it comes from refusing to let every problem have unlimited access to your mind.

That is a different kind of strength.

It means you notice what needs attention, respond to what requires action, and then release what cannot be solved tonight.

That last part is important.

Some things cannot be solved tonight.

Not the student's home life.
Not the long email chain.
Not the weak lesson from earlier.

Not the deeper school problem.
Not the whole weight of the profession.

Teachers do not need to carry unresolved things all evening just because they are unresolved.

Sometimes the strongest thing you can do is say:

This is important, but I am not carrying it all night.

That sentence has saved me more than once.

Because peace does not hold itself.
You have to guard it.

And in this profession, if you do not do that on purpose, the job will keep reaching for it.

What I Learned

I learned that bringing the job home is not only about workload. It is also about mental and emotional carryover. Once I started protecting my evenings more carefully, I became more present at home and more grounded at school.

Why This Works

Teachers need real recovery in order to stay patient, clear-headed, and effective. Boundaries do not make a teacher less caring. They help a teacher last longer and show up better the next day.

Try This Tomorrow

Before you leave school, choose one simple closing step:

- make tomorrow's short to-do list

- answer only the email that truly cannot wait
- leave grading at school
- say to yourself, *I did enough for today*

End the day on purpose.

My Next Move

What am I still carrying home that does not actually need my time or energy tonight?

____

____

____

____

If You Want to Go Deeper: *Angela Watson's Fewer Things, Better offers a helpful framework for reducing overwhelm, protecting your energy, and making more sustainable decisions as a teacher. It is especially useful for teachers who struggle with overworking, overcommitting, or feeling like the job is expanding into every part of their lives.*

Chapter 19
Be Effective Without Being Perfect

If you have read this far, I want you to hear something clearly:

You do not have to be perfect to be a good teacher.

You do not have to handle every moment flawlessly. You do not have to respond to every disruption with the right words at the right time. You do not have to build a classroom where nothing ever goes wrong, no student ever pushes back, and every lesson lands the way you planned it.

That classroom does not exist.

And chasing it will exhaust you faster than any difficult class ever could.

What I have learned, after years of teaching in real classrooms with real students, is that the teachers who last are not the ones who got everything right.

They are the ones who became clear enough and grounded enough to keep leading even when things were messy.

That is the difference.

Not perfection.

Clarity.

Clarity about what you expect.
Clarity about how you respond.
Clarity about what you will and will not accept.
Clarity about where your job ends and the rest of your life begins.

That kind of clarity does not come from reading one book, attending one training, or having one good week. It comes from doing the work, reflecting honestly, adjusting when something is not working, and refusing to let a bad day become your permanent identity as a teacher.

I wrote this book because I remember what it felt like to stand in front of a class and not know whether I was doing anything right. I remember the Sunday-night dread. I remember the frustration of repeating myself all day and still feeling like nothing changed. I remember thinking that other teachers must have something I did not.

They did not.

They just had more clarity.

They knew what their room should look like. They taught expectations on purpose. They followed through without waiting for perfection. They built routines that carried the weight so their emotions did not have to. They contacted parents before things spiraled. They kept records. They asked for help when they needed it. They protected their own time without guilt.

None of that required perfection.

It required honesty about what works and what does not.

That is what I have tried to give you in these pages.

Not a list of things to memorize.
Not a set of scripts to follow exactly.
Not a picture of some flawless classroom you are supposed to replicate.

Just the truth about what helped me, told as clearly as I know how.

Some of it you will use right away.
Some of it will click later.
Some of it you will adapt to fit your own room, your own students, and your own voice.

That is how it should work.

Because this book was never meant to turn you into someone else.

It was meant to help you become a calmer, clearer, more grounded version of yourself in the classroom.

That is the version your students need.

Not the version who never makes mistakes.
The version who recovers well.

Not the version who controls every second of the day.
The version who leads with enough structure that the room does not depend on luck.

Not the version who has all the answers.
The version who is honest enough to keep learning.

I have seen teachers walk into rooms where nothing was working and slowly turn them around. Not because they found one magic strategy, but because they stopped guessing and started building. They taught expectations. They tightened routines. They followed through calmly. They connected with students without abandoning structure. They gave themselves permission to reset, to reteach, and to start again.

That is real teaching.

It is not glamorous.
It is not always rewarding in the moment.
Some weeks it barely feels survivable.

But it is honest work.

And honest work builds something that lasts.

So if you are still struggling, that does not mean you are in the wrong profession.

It may mean no one taught you the things that actually hold a classroom together. It may mean you have been trying to build a room on relationships alone without enough structure. It may mean you have been reacting all day instead of leading. It may mean you need better systems, not more willpower.

Those are fixable things.

And fixing them does not require being the best teacher in the building. It requires being clear enough to lead your room, honest enough to reflect on what is not working, and grounded enough to keep going when it is hard.

You can do that.

Not perfectly.
But clearly.

And clearly is enough.

If there is one thing I want you to take from this book, it is this:

Your classroom does not need a perfect teacher.
It needs a clear one.

A teacher who means what they say.
A teacher who builds routines that make the day feel steadier.
A teacher who protects the learning environment without losing themselves in the process.

That kind of teaching is not about having all the answers. It is about showing up, paying attention, adjusting when needed, and staying grounded enough to keep going.

Some days will still be hard. Some classes will still test you. Some moments will still leave you wondering what you could have done better.

That does not mean you are doing it wrong.
It means you are teaching.

This work gets lighter when your classroom starts to make more sense—when expectations are clearer, routines are stronger, and you are no longer carrying every part of the day by yourself.

That is what I hope this book gives you.

Not perfection.
Not pressure.
Just something solid to come back to when the job feels heavy.

And if it helps you walk into your classroom a little calmer, a little clearer, and a little more sure of your next step, then let that be enough.

You can do this.

Recommended Resources

These are books I have found genuinely useful—not because they are perfect, but because they offer practical ideas that hold up in real classrooms. You do not need to read all of them. Pick the one that speaks most to where you are right now.

On Procedures and the First Days of School

Wong, H. K., & Wong, R. T. (1998). *The First Days of School: How to Be an Effective Teacher.* Harry K. Wong Publications.
This book is a strong foundation for understanding why procedures matter so much. It is especially helpful for new teachers and for anyone whose classroom feels disorganized or unclear.

On Specific Teaching Techniques

Lemov, D. (2010). *Teach Like a Champion: 49 Techniques That Put Students on the Path to College.* Jossey-Bass.
This book offers concrete, named techniques for everything from transitions to checking for understanding. It is detailed, specific, and action-oriented. Even reading a few chapters can change the way you run your classroom.

On Classroom Management Systems

Jones, F. (2007). *Tools for Teaching.* Fredric H. Jones & Associates.
Jones focuses on body language, movement, and systems that reduce disruption without relying too heavily on verbal correction. His approach is especially helpful for teachers who feel like they are talking too much.

Sprick, R. (2009). *CHAMPs: A Proactive and Positive Approach to Classroom Management* (2nd ed.). Pacific Northwest Publishing.
This book is especially helpful for teachers who want a clear system for teaching expectations, structuring routines, and preventing disruption before it starts. It provides practical language and concrete tools for building a calmer, more predictable classroom.

On Assertive Discipline and Follow-Through

Canter, L. (2010). *Assertive Discipline: Positive Behavior Management for Today's Classroom* (4th ed.). Solution Tree Press.
This book helps clarify the difference between being passive, being hostile, and being assertive. It is a useful resource for teachers who struggle with consistency and follow-through.

On Understanding Difficult Behavior

Greene, R. W. (2008). *Lost at School: Why Our Kids with Behavioral Challenges Are Falling Through the Cracks and How We Can Help Them.* Scribner.
Greene's framework offers a more compassionate and structured way to understand students whose behavior does not respond to typical management strategies.

On Classroom Management as a Craft

Bennett, T. (2020). *Running the Room: The Teacher's Guide to Behaviour.* John Catt Educational.
This book treats classroom management as a skill you can study and refine rather than something based on personality. The advice is practical and grounded in real experience.

On Research-Based Strategies

Marzano, R. J., Marzano, J. S., & Pickering, D. J. (2003). *Classroom Management That Works: Research-Based Strategies for Every Teacher.* ASCD.

This resource connects classroom management to research in a way that is both accessible and actionable.

On Teacher Sustainability and Reducing Overwhelm

Watson, A. (2019). *Fewer Things, Better: The Courage to Focus on What Matters Most.* Due Season Press and Educational Services.

This book supports teachers in reducing overwhelm and making more intentional decisions about time, workload, and priorities.

On Simplicity, Responsibility, and Classroom Ownership

Linsin, M. (2009). *The Classroom Management Secret: And 45 Other Keys to a Well-Behaved Class.* JME Press.

Linsin offers direct and practical advice for building a calm classroom through clarity, consistency, and student responsibility.

About the Author

Xiomara Granado-Ramos, M.Ed., is an educator with more than six years of experience working with diverse learners across grade levels, including adults. Originally from Carolina, Puerto Rico, she currently teaches middle school in San Antonio, Texas, while also providing professional development in her school district on topics such as classroom management, student engagement, student-centered instruction, curriculum, and other areas of instructional practice.

What shapes her work most is that she is still in the classroom. She still experiences the daily realities of teaching—the routines, the interruptions, the challenging moments, the resets, and the small wins that make the work meaningful. She does not write from theory alone or from a distance. She writes from lived experience.

Through both her teaching and her training, Xiomara is passionate about helping educators build classrooms that feel clear, calm, and manageable without becoming harsh, performative, or overwhelmed. Her goal is to offer teachers practical strategies they can use right away, especially in the often challenging middle school and early high school years.

She lives with her husband and two children and continues to teach, learn, and remind herself daily that clarity matters more than perfection.

www.ingramcontent.com/pod-product-compliance
Lightning Source LLC
LaVergne TN
LVHW090513110826
845146LV00003B/842

* 9 7 9 8 9 8 7 5 4 6 9 8 7 *